# PASS YOUR TEST WITH MOTORCYCLE CITY

## foulsham

LONDON • NEW YORK • TORONTO • SYDNEY

# foulsham

The Publishing House, Bennetts Close, Cippenham,
Slough, Berkshire, SL1 5AP, England

ISBN 0–572–02518-1

Text copyright © 2000 Motorcycle City

Artwork copyright © 2000 W. Foulsham & Co. Ltd

While every effort has been made to ensure the accuracy of all
the information contained within this book, neither the authors
nor the publisher can be liable for any errors. In particular, since
laws change from time to time, it is vital that each individual
should check relevant legal details for themselves.

Printed in Malaysia.

# CONTENTS

Introduction                                          7

Chapter 1    What Makes a Good Rider?                 9

Chapter 2    The Importance of Training              17

Chapter 3    Which Bike?                             19

Chapter 4    The Law                                 29

Chapter 5    Compulsory Basic Training               39

             *Module A*                              41

             *Module B*                              49

             *Module C*                              67

             *Module D*                              87

             *Module E*                             101

Chapter 6    Further Training                        103

Chapter 7    The Direct Access Scheme                143

Chapter 8    The Motorcycle Test                     147

             Motorcycling Terms and Abbreviations    154

             Index                                   157

Riding a motorcycle is great fun and is enjoyed by people of all ages for many different reasons. Some use motorcycles because they can be economical and make short work of city traffic, others because they enjoy the freedom a motorcycle gives, coupled with high performance for relatively low cost. Some go for the image of the laid-back cruiser, and all enjoy the companionship shared with other enthusiasts.

This book draws on the experience of many dedicated instructors, and is written to help the new rider avoid the most common mistakes made by learners. Read this book in conjunction with good professional training. Reading it before you start your training will prepare you for the challenges ahead.

Motorcycle City Training is one of the largest professional motorcycle training companies in the UK – and is a division of the UK's number one motorcycle dealership. We provide a complete service for the learner rider from Compulsory Basic Training (CBT) to test-standard training on small and large motorcycles. We tailor courses to suit the customer and provide motorcycles for hire and free use of safety helmets and waterproofs. Many of the courses are guaranteed, which means that if a customer fails the motorcycle test, any further tuition is provided free of charge.

All our rider training centres are at permanent sites, most within our showrooms, and offer training seven days per week (office hours). All instructors are trained to the highest standards and approved by the Driving Standards Agency (DSA). Our aim is to train motorcyclists to ride safely for life and not just to pass the test.

Once a customer has passed the motorcycle test, we can provide further training in the form of our Riding Dynamics course. Run in conjunction with Brands Hatch Leisure Group, this is a three-day course that includes two days on-road together with one day on-track training. This advanced course will enhance a rider's skill and confidence and help them get the most out of their motorcycling. Our back-to-biking course is ideal for those returning to a bike after a break from two wheels.

Motorcycling attracts people of both sexes, young and old, from the rich and famous to the poverty-stricken student or wide-eyed teenager. Anyone riding in today's traffic needs to carefully consider their attitude towards motorcycling in general and safe riding habits in particular. To become a good rider, you will need to work hard to perfect the following skills.

## CONCENTRATION

Riding on today's busy roads is demanding and requires absolute concentration. A lapse in concentration may lead to a nasty fright – or something worse.

The ability to concentrate is a skill that must be learnt and, as with any other form of skill, learning it can be very tiring. Learner riders tire easily in the early stages of training, but this gets better as their concentration improves. The learner rider should keep to short journeys. Brief commutes or pleasure trips are fine, but no intercity or long-haul treks!

Our ability to process information about our surroundings is limited, and a rider should be aware of this. A good rider will scan the surroundings to gain as much information as possible about potential hazards. A rider who concentrates on too small an area is likely to miss a hazard.

### Things that Can Disrupt Concentration

#### Anger or Impatience
Commonly known as 'road rage'. An angry rider is likely to concentrate on the alleged wrongdoer, to the exclusion of all other hazards. A rider who jumps on a motorcycle after a family row is not likely to be concentrating on riding safely.

### Personal Worries

Worrying about the gas or phone bill, or about getting there on time, means a rider is more likely to miss a hazard.

### Fatigue or Illness

Working long hours and then trying to ride a motorcycle is not recommended. Motorcycling is more tiring than driving a car because riders are exposed to the additional factors of noise, vibration, wind and weather. Feeling unwell is guaranteed to affect concentration.

### Drink and Drugs

Consuming even small amounts of alcohol will affect concentration and increase reaction times. The only sensible advice is do not drink and ride. Prohibited drugs have the same debilitating effects as alcohol, and even prescription drugs from a doctor or patent medicines from a pharmacist can have unwanted side effects such as drowsiness. If in doubt, don't ride.

### Weather

The cold and wet will affect concentration levels. A good rider always dresses appropriately and stays comfortable, dry and warm.

## GOOD OBSERVATIONS

Good observations aid anticipation and are essential for survival. A motorcyclist sits higher and has a better view than many drivers, and can take advantage of this in driving safely.

### Field of View

The area a rider can see from the riding position is known as the 'field of view'. As the rider travels along the road, the field of view is constantly changing. The field of view will be one of the considerations governing the rider's speed. If the field of view reduces, a rider should slow down and even be prepared to stop.

When approaching junctions the initial view is often poor, but as the rider approaches the view opens out. Objects such as parked vehicles, trees, hedges and lamp posts can restrict the field of view, and in such cases a rider must be careful, edging forward until the view improves.

## Focused Observations

When making observations, it is important to allow time for the eyes to focus. If the eyes don't focus properly, it is impossible to assess accurately critical factors such as speed and distance.

## Rear Observations

It is important to be aware of what's happening behind you at all times. The view through the mirrors of a motorcycle is usually very restricted, with large blind spots. Turning the head to look behind allows a rider to check the blind spots, and gives a better idea of the speed and distance of following traffic.

It is possible to spend too much time looking behind – why look twice when once would do? It is essential to consider the timing: for example, what would happen if a rider looked behind just as a vehicle began emerging from a junction in front? The rider must therefore make sure that they look behind often enough but not too often, and at the right times. Effective rear observations should be made before moving off, slowing down, stopping, accelerating, changing position, turning, or on the approach to any hazard.

## Lifesaver Observations

A lifesaver look is a final glance into the relevant blind spot before moving position or turning. It is taken in the direction of the move or turn, and needs to be done early enough to take avoiding action if necessary.

## Scanning

Good riders scan their surrounding in all directions; their eyes sweep the foreground, middle and far distance, to the sides and the rear. A rider who scans repeatedly is more likely to spot potential hazards. Mirrors should be used regularly and, if necessary, in conjunction with rear observations to complete the overall picture.

## GOOD HAZARD SPOTTING

A hazard is anything potentially dangerous to a motorcyclist. It could be blatantly obvious, such as a lorry emerging from a junction on the left, or it could be potentially dangerous, such as parked vehicles obscuring the view into a junction. A good rider will recognise hazards or potentially dangerous situations and deal with them promptly by taking the appropriate actions.

Appropriate actions may include slowing down or stopping, moving position, sounding the horn, turning or accelerating. If a rider fails to spot a hazard the appropriate actions cannot be taken, and an accident may be the unfortunate result.

## The Three Main Categories of Hazard

- Road features such as junctions, bends, crossings or roundabouts.
- Hazards caused by the position or action of other road users.
- Hazards caused by differing road surfaces or the weather conditions.

A rider must be able to prioritise hazards according to the level of threat. There is little point worrying too much about the pedestrian at the kerbside in the distance if a car is pulling out directly in front of you!

## ALERTNESS AND ANTICIPATION

Good anticipation gives a rider more time to react to a hazard, and to anticipate well a rider must be wide awake and alert. The ability to anticipate events correctly depends very much on training and the rider's own experience.

### Examples of How Good Anticipation Can Help a Rider

A ball bounces out into the road; what can be expected to happen next?

The rider knows a child will probably appear in the road, so slows down. Sure enough the child runs out after the ball, and the rider has avoided a nasty accident.

The traffic lights have been on green for ages; what will happen next?

The rider anticipates the change to red and slows down a little earlier on the approach. Sure enough the lights change, and the rider stops smoothly and safely behind the stop line.

Alertness is essential for good anticipation and is closely linked to concentration. The factors previously listed under 'Concentration' will also affect alertness.

## FORWARD PLANNING

Skilful riders plan well ahead, using good observations, concentration, alertness and anticipation. All the information received is used to formulate a riding plan. The rider works continually to anticipate hazards, prioritise them and decide what course of action best suits the situation. The planning never stops; as soon as the conditions change, the plan changes.

### Aspects to be Considered

- The actions or likely actions of other road users.

- What the rider can and cannot see.

- The existing road conditions.

## PATIENCE

Patience is something many drivers and riders seem to have lost completely. The heavier the traffic, the more impatient people become; it seems to be an in-built reaction. A good rider works hard at being patient and considerate, even though it's not always easy! If another road user drives or behaves badly, don't be tempted to retaliate or intimidate them by riding erratically or too close.

### Road Rage

This is the current buzz term for anger and impatience. It's nothing new: it has always been around, there's just more of it as the roads become more crowded. Losing your temper and retaliating will usually solicit a similar response from the alleged wrongdoer and the incident can escalate to ridiculous proportions – people have been run over, stabbed or even shot as a result.

If a rider 'loses it' and concentrates solely on revenge, all other hazards fade into the background and something unpleasant is often the outcome.

The intelligent rider avoids self-inflicted pressures and sets off in plenty of time to avoid rushing. Be courteous and considerate, don't judge others harshly and remember that everyone makes mistakes occasionally.

## DEFENSIVE ATTITUDE

Riders who avoid accidents expect the unexpected and assume nothing. They always question the intentions of other road users and learn from experience. Remember the old expression 'familiarity breeds contempt' – just because there has never previously been a queue of traffic around a particular bend doesn't mean there isn't one now!

## GOOD MACHINE CONTROL

The best riders have practised long and hard to master the controls of a motorcycle. It is essential to develop good co-ordination of hands and feet together with balance, sight, sound and smell. Riding a motorcycle safely is a complex skill made up of many smaller skills.

A novice rider will initially concentrate hard on mastering these skills, and good training will spend a lot of time on basic machine control. As a rider becomes more confident in the use of the controls, more time will be given to concentrating on the road conditions.

There is no substitute for experience: practice makes perfect and effective, well-planned training makes it even better.

## RESPONSIBILITY

Good riders strive to develop a positive safe attitude. They are aware of their own vulnerability and know their own and their machine's limitations. They are tolerant and considerate and work towards developing a high degree of safety for themselves and others. These qualities provide the key to skilful, enjoyable riding.

Acquiring any complex skill requires good training and regular practice. Statistically, riders who receive training are much less likely to be involved in an accident. Just reading this book will not make you a good rider; you need to get yourself along to a good motorcycle training school and practise hard and long to develop the skills and judgement required to survive on today's roads.

## WHO CAN PROVIDE TRAINING?

Motorcycle training such as Compulsory Basic Training (CBT) and the Direct Access Scheme (DAS) can only be provided by training establishments approved by the Driving Standards Agency (DSA). These companies are known as Approved Training Bodies (ATBs). Instructors working for an ATB will have attended a DSA assessment and will hold Certificates of Authorisation to conduct CBT or DAS training. Before approval, the company's premises will have been inspected to ensure a safe training environment for novice riders.

## CHOOSING A TRAINING BODY

Training bodies come in all shapes and sizes, from one-man bands to national companies. It pays to shop around – what suits someone else may not suit you. If you have friends who are motorcyclists, ask them where they trained as they may be able to recommend a company. Check the *Yellow Pages* and *Thomson Local* directories.

Make sure they have adequate premises, with classroom facilities and a suitable off-road training area. Check that the motorcycles and radios suit your requirements and that the instructors are professional and well presented. Most training companies have learner motorcycles for hire. Safety helmets, gloves and waterproofs are usually provided free of charge.

If you decide to book a course of tuition, make sure you know exactly how many hours of training you will receive and that the fee you are paying includes such things as motorcycle hire, comprehensive insurance cover and any test fees.

In the end the choice is yours. Don't be rushed or pressured into parting with your hard-earned cash. Take your time and be absolutely certain that you have made the right choice for you.

If you use your own motorcycle for training, make sure it's 'learner legal' (see 'Types of Bike' below) and roadworthy. If you're hiring a machine from your training school you need to consider carefully which motorcycle best suits your needs once you've passed the test.

## YOUR BUDGET

As well as the initial purchase price of the machine, you must take into account the additional cost of a safety helmet and clothing, insurance, road tax, fuel and general running and maintenance costs.

## TAKE ADVICE

Visit your local motorcycle dealers and explain your requirements and listen to their advice, ask your friends and speak to your instructor. Read the road-test reports in the motorcycle press and consider all this information before making a final decision. There's nothing worse than buying a new bike and finding it doesn't suit you.

## TYPES OF BIKE

The following outline descriptions of the main types of bike available should help you make your choice of a suitable bike.

### *Mopeds*

- Have an engine capacity of 50 cc or less.

- Are restricted to a maximum speed of 50 kph (31 mph).

- Don't weigh more than 250 kg.

- Can be moved by pedals if registered before 1 August 1977.

- Are available with manual gears or automatic transmission.

Mopeds are very popular and can be ridden solo by anyone aged 16 or over who holds a provisional licence and has completed CBT. L-plates must be displayed (or D-plates in Wales). Full car, motorcycle or moped licence holders may ride a moped and carry a pillion passenger without displaying L-plates; however, note that this will soon change (see page 37).

## Learner-legal Motorcycles

- Have an engine capacity of 125 cc or less.

- The engine power output does not exceed 11 kW (14.6 bhp).

- Have manual gears.

The above engine size and power output restrictions do not apply to Direct Access Scheme learners (see Chapter 7).

These machines are economical and compact. They are designed for commuting and short journeys and are a favourite with learners.

Learners must:

- Display L-plates (or D-plates in Wales).

- Not carry a pillion passenger.

## Automatics

- Have engine sizes ranging from 50 cc to 400 cc.

- Have automatic gear-changing.

- Give good protection from wind and weather.

- Are compact, comfortable and very easy to use.

- Are economical to run.

If you take your test on one of these, your full-licence entitlement will be restricted to automatics; the usual learner restrictions will apply if you ride a manual-geared machine, unless you take a further test.

These machines are great for short journeys and for commuting in heavy town traffic.

## Scooters and Commuters

- Generally have an engine size from 50 cc to 125 cc.

- Have automatic or semi-automatic gear-changing.

- Are specifically designed for commuting to and from work or the shops.

- Are very economical to run.

- Are lightweight and very manoeuvrable.

## Sports Bikes

- Have engine sizes from 50 cc to 1300 cc.

- Are generally more expensive to buy and run.

- Are capable of very high speeds.

- Can have an uncomfortable riding position, almost lying flat in some cases.

The 'Pocket Rocket' or sports replica, with cutting-edge, road-racer styling: riding these machines safely requires considerable skill, and novices should take great care. They are designed for high-speed fun on fast roads and can be agony about town.

## Tourers

- Have a large engine tuned for touring, ranging from 500 cc to 1500 cc.

- Have a comfortable riding position for both rider and pillion passenger.

- Are generally fitted with luggage racks for panniers and top boxes.

- Are often fitted with a full fairing and windscreen.

These are comfy long-haul motorcycles, designed to cruise at motorway speeds carrying a pillion passenger and luggage.

## Custom Cruisers

- Are available in a wide range of engine sizes from 125 cc to 1500 cc.

- Hard-tail models have a rigid frame with no rear suspension.

- Most have a very low seat height.

These motorcycles have American 'heavy-metal' styling, with lots of chrome and a laid-back, feet-forward riding position.

## Off-Roaders (Trail Bikes)

- Have engine sizes from 50 cc to 1000 cc.

- Have extra ground clearance.

- Have a high seat height.

- Are usually fitted with dual-purpose tyres to permit use on varying surfaces while remaining road-legal.

Trail bikes have a dual purpose: they can be used both on and off-road. They are designed for 'green laning' (riding on unmade roads, tracks and lanes) and riding over uneven ground.

## BUYING A BIKE

### *Buying New*

It is often possible to find a deal which will include such extras as insurance cover, a safety helmet and clothing. Make sure you understand the fine details of any warranty or guarantee. Again it will be down to your personal preference; some dealers will offer low prices but restricted after-sales service, while others may be more expensive initially but may provide good after-sales service.

### *Buying Second-hand*

If you're buying second-hand it's best to take along someone who knows about bikes and listen to their advice. Take your time and thoroughly check the bike for damage; if the mirrors, handlebar ends, exhaust or fairing are scratched, this means the bike has been dropped at some time. Check the engine and frame numbers match those in the registration document. You can check that the bike is not stolen or has outstanding hire-purchase payments by phoning any of the companies who conduct these checks.

Before riding a motorcycle as a learner on public roads you must comply with certain legal requirements. If you ride illegally, don't be surprised when your licence starts sprouting penalty points and your bank balance disappears! You may even find yourself disqualified or imprisoned.

## ESSENTIAL DOCUMENTS

### Driving Licence

You must have a valid UK licence, whether it's a provisional licence or a full licence with provisional motorcycle entitlement. It must show your correct name, address and personal details, and must be signed.

### Insurance

You must have a current certificate of insurance or a valid cover note for the machine you are using. Riding without insurance is a serious offence. Cover can be arranged through an insurance company or broker. Sometimes insurance can be arranged through your motorcycle dealer or through the manufacturer.

Shop around for the best deal, always read the small print and make sure you have the cover you want.

There are three main types of insurance cover.

### Third Party Only

The third party is any person you might injure or whose property you might damage; this includes any pillion passenger. You won't be covered for any personal injury or damage to your own motorcycle or property, whatever the cause.

*Third Party, Fire and Theft*

This provides the same third-party cover but also provides cover if your motorcycle is stolen or damaged by fire.

*Comprehensive*

This is probably the best insurance cover but it is also the most expensive, and certain classes of rider may be unable to get this type of cover. These policies will cover you for all the previous liabilities as well as personal injury and damage to your machine. As with all insurance policies, there will be certain conditions and exclusions, particularly in relation to where the bike is parked when not in use.

## Vehicle Test Certificate

The Ministry of Transport test, or MOT, applies to all motorcycles over three years old from the date of first registration. The test must be conducted at an approved vehicle testing station; many motorcycle dealers are approved testers. Its purpose is to test the motorcycle's basic roadworthiness, but it is not a guarantee that a machine is legal or roadworthy; faults can and will develop between tests. It is the owner's and rider's responsibility to ensure that a machine is legal, roadworthy and safe.

## Registration Document (V5)

This document, often referred to as the 'logbook', contains details of the owner's name and address, the vehicle's registration number, make, model and colour, engine size and number.

When you buy or sell a motorcycle or change address you must inform the Driver and Vehicle Licensing Agency (DVLA) immediately.

## Vehicle Excise Duty

Although this is commonly called 'road tax', in fact these days it has little to do with the upkeep of the roads – it's a tax on the ownership of a vehicle. You must display the Vehicle Excise Licence, or tax disc, clearly on the vehicle. On a motorcycle it should be displayed on the front left-hand side of the machine, forward of the engine. Failure to display the licence disc correctly is an offence.

The fee will vary with engine size. The categories are: up to 150 cc; 151 to 250 cc; over 250 cc.

### Tax-exempt Motorcycles
Some motorcycles over 25 years old may be tax-exempt, but they must still display a 'nil duty' licence disc.

### Statutory Off-Road Notification (SORN)
If a motorcycle is to be kept off-road and not be taxed, the registered keeper must complete and submit a SORN stating where the machine is kept.

## CBT Certificate (DL196)

To ride on public roads, a learner must have satisfactorily completed Compulsory Basic Training (CBT) and hold a Certificate of Completion issued by an Approved Training Body. This certificate validates the provisional moped or motorcycle entitlement on the learner's licence. The certificate presently lasts for three years, although there are moves afoot to reduce this to two years (see page 37). If a learner has not taken and passed the test within that time, CBT must be completed again.

**DSA**
SAFE DRIVING FOR LIFE

1164404

Road Traffic Act 1988

### Certificate of Completion of an Approved Training Course for Motor Vehicles in Categories A and P

Driver Number of Candidate

Hrs    Mins

Date and Time of Course Completion

Current Name

Current Address

Postcode

has successfully completed an approved training course for motor vehicles in categories A and P, prescribed for the purpose of Section 97 of the Road Traffic Act 1988 as amended by Section 6 of the Road Traffic (Driver Licensing and Information Systems) Act 1989.

Signature of Instructor

Appointed to conduct such training

Initials and surname (BLOCK CAPITALS)

No.

**The successful candidate should sign in ink below in the presence of the instructor.**

**Signature**

Address of site at which Course conducted

Official Stamp of Training Body

MOTORCYCLE CITY TRAINING
149-151 LYNCHFORD ROAD
FARNBOROUGH
HANTS
GU14 6HG

Site No.

**Please read the notes overleaf**

An Executive Agency of the  *DETR*
Department
Environment
Transport
Regions

DL 196
Rev (08/99)

## L-plates

Learner riders must display L-plates of the correct size and colour (a red 'L' on a white background) to the front and rear of the motorcycle. They should be displayed vertically and flat, and must not be cut down or wrapped around the suspension or mudguard.

D-plates may be displayed in Wales (the term for learner in Welsh is 'Dysgwr').

Green L-plates are for those who have recently passed the test.

## GAINING A LICENCE

The flowcharts on the following pages will help you to navigate your way to a full licence.

Further details of the procedures shown here are given in later chapters.

The flowcharts have been reproduced with the permission of the Department of the Environment, Transport and the Regions.

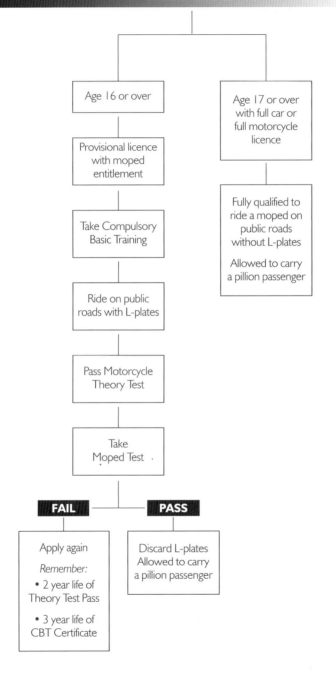

# MOPEDS

**Age 16 or over**

**Provisional licence with moped entitlement**

**Take Compulsory Basic Training**

**Ride on public roads with L-plates**

**Pass Motorcycle Theory Test**

**Take Moped Test**

**FAIL**

Apply again

*Remember:*

• 2 year life of Theory Test Pass

• 3 year life of CBT Certificate

**PASS**

Discard L-plates
Allowed to carry
a pillion passenger

**Age 17 or over with full car or full motorcycle licence**

Fully qualified to ride a moped on public roads without L-plates

Allowed to carry a pillion passenger

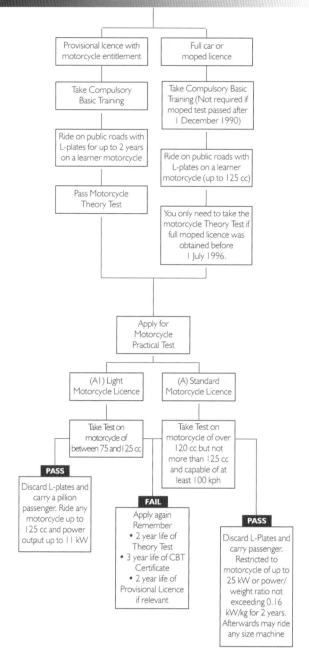

# MOTORCYCLES

Provisional lcence with motorcycle entitlement

Full car or moped licence

Take Compulsory Basic Training

Take Compulsory Basic Training (Not required if moped test passed after 1 December 1990)

Ride on public roads with L-plates for up to 2 years on a learner motorcycle

Ride on public roads with L-plates on a learner motorcycle (up to 125 cc)

Pass Motorcycle Theory Test

You only need to take the motorcycle Theory Test if full moped licence was obtained before 1 July 1996.

Apply for Motorcycle Practical Test

(A1) Light Motorcycle Licence

(A) Standard Motorcycle Licence

Take Test on motorcycle of between 75 and 125 cc

Take Test on motorcycle of over 120 cc but not more than 125 cc and capable of at least 100 kph

**PASS**

Discard L-plates and carry a pillion passenger. Ride any motorcycle up to 125 cc and power output up to 11 kW

**FAIL**

Apply again Remember
• 2 year life of Theory Test
• 3 year life of CBT Certificate
• 2 year life of Provisional Licence if relevant

**PASS**

Discard L-Plates and carry passenger. Restricted to motorcycle of up to 25 kW or power/weight ratio not exceeding 0.16 kW/kg for 2 years. Afterwards may ride any size machine

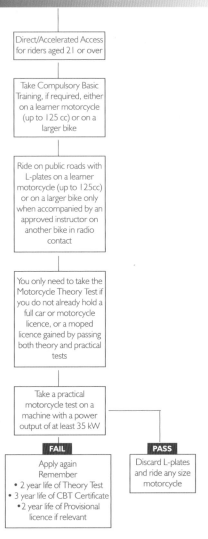

Direct/Accelerated Access for riders aged 21 or over

Take Compulsory Basic Training, if required, either on a learner motorcycle (up to 125 cc) or on a larger bike

Ride on public roads with L-plates on a learner motorcycle (up to 125cc) or on a larger bike only when accompanied by an approved instructor on another bike in radio contact

You only need to take the Motorcycle Theory Test if you do not already hold a full car or motorcycle licence, or a moped licence gained by passing both theory and practical tests

Take a practical motorcycle test on a machine with a power output of at least 35 kW

**FAIL**

Apply again
Remember
• 2 year life of Theory Test
• 3 year life of CBT Certificate
• 2 year life of Provisional licence if relevant

**PASS**

Discard L-plates and ride any size motorcycle

Changes will be taking place in late 2000. The following proposals are under discussion:

- The CBT certificate will only be valid for two years.

- New car licence holders will lose their automatic entitlement to ride mopeds.

- Provisional licences may cover all categories with no two-year restriction on the motorcycle entitlement.

- A separate theory test will be required for each category of vehicle.

So you've checked it all out and decided you want to go for it – welcome to the club! Your first step will be Compulsory Basic Training (CBT); turn up at the appointed time and place and get stuck in. Here are a few tips to help you on your way.

## WHAT TO TAKE
### *Driving Licence*

You must take this; your instructor will want to see it as you cannot complete the on-road elements of CBT without producing a valid licence. Make sure it's signed and has the correct entitlement.

### *Your Motorcycle*

If you intend using your own machine it will have to be delivered to the training site. Make sure it has proper L-plates front and rear and that it's taxed, roadworthy and legal.

### *Documents*

If you are using your own machine, take along the registration document (V5), your insurance certificate or cover note and your MOT certificate (if required).

## WHAT TO WEAR

Not everyone will want to turn up in full leathers, but you must dress sensibly with the emphasis on protection, as even a small spill on the training pad can result in bruises and grazes. Sturdy outdoor clothing with a jacket and jeans will suffice; do not wear skiing kit as it gives little protection. Wear boots that protect the ankle, and tuck any laces out of the way.

Most training centres provide helmets and waterproofs, but if you have your own take them along.

If you normally wear glasses or contact lenses take them with you; you'll need them for the eyesight test and whilst riding.

## THE STRUCTURE OF A CBT COURSE

The course is divided into five modules and a learner must satisfactorily complete each module in a set order before being issued with a Certificate of Completion. For instance a learner may not begin Module B before satisfactorily completing Module A.

The modules are as follows:

**MODULE A: Introduction**

**MODULE B: Practical on-site training**

**MODULE C: Practical on-site riding**

**MODULE D: Practical on-road training**

**MODULE E: Practical on-road riding**

## MODULE A: Introduction

This section will usually be done in a classroom environment, particularly important if the weather is bad!

### EYESIGHT CHECK

Before starting any training your instructor will check your eyesight. If you normally wear glasses or contact lenses you will be able to use them for the test and you must use them whilst riding.

In good daylight you must be able to read a normal-sized registration plate (letters and figures 79.4 mm/3.1 in high) at a minimum distance of 20.5 m (about 67 ft).

Your instructor will then give you informative talks about the aims of CBT, equipment and clothing. Make sure you pay attention as they are very important topics.

### THE AIMS OF THE CBT COURSE

CBT was introduced in December 1990 to help reduce the quite appalling accident rate among learner riders. Since its introduction the accident rate has been considerably reduced.

### THE IMPORTANCE OF USING THE CORRECT EQUIPMENT AND CLOTHING

Your instructor will have good examples of equipment and clothing to illustrate these talks.

## The Motorcycle Safety Helmet

Motorcyclists must wear an approved safety helmet when riding on public roads.

### British Standard

Safety helmets must display a British Standards Institute (BSI) kite-mark sticker, either the blue Type A or the green Type B. Both will have reached BS6658; the Type A will have been tested to a higher standard. Do not purchase or use a helmet that does not show a kite-mark or its equivalent as it may be sub-standard and offer inadequate protection in the event of an accident.

### European Standard

Safety helmets must comply to a European standard at least equivalent to the British Standard (BS6658) and carry a mark equivalent to the BSI kite-mark.

### Full-face Helmets

These give better facial protection than an open-face helmet, and with an integral visor they also protect from wind, rain and insects. Some people feel closed in by this type of helmet; because of the chinbar they can be quite heavy and can restrict a rider's view.

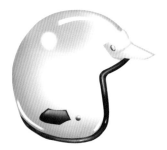

### Open-face Helmets

These give little facial protection and should always be used with goggles or a clip-on visor for eye protection. They tend to weigh less than the full-face version and give the rider a good view.

### Helmet Construction

A helmet is constructed of a hard outer shell of polycarbonate or fibreglass (the fibreglass may be mixed with other strong lightweight materials such as carbon fibre or Kevlar). Inside this is a thick inner liner of expanded polystyrene foam, which in turn is lined with foam and fabric for comfort.

### One Impact

Safety helmets are one-impact devices. If a helmet suffers a heavy impact the compressible inner liner may be damaged, and this damage may not be obvious from the outside. The helmet should be discarded (preferably with the straps cut to prevent others from using it) and replaced with a new one.

### Personal Use

Helmets are a personal item and should not be lent or borrowed. To a certain extent, a helmet moulds to the shape of your head and it is unlikely to fit anyone else properly.

### Buying a Helmet

Shop around and try as many makes and sizes as possible to make sure you have a good fit. A helmet should fit snugly and not be too tight or loose; it will bed in somewhat and mould itself to the shape of your head. Never buy second-hand: you don't know the helmet's history, it may be damaged.

## Fasteners

When you wear a helmet, it should always be fastened properly under your chin. There are three main types of fastening: the double D-ring, the bar and buckle, and the quick-release.

Double D-ring                          Bar and buckle

Quick-release

## Stickers and Painting

Follow the manufacturer's advice about stickers and painting a helmet as the solvents in adhesives and paint can damage the shell.

## Cleaning

Use only mild detergents and warm water, never solvents or bleaches as these will damage the shell. You can buy proprietary cleaners for the lining.

### Lifespan and General Care

The lifespan of a helmet will depend on care and usage. Look after it and use a helmet bag and it will last longer than one that's been left around the floor! Use of a helmet bag will prevent accidental scratching of the helmet and visor. Don't place your helmet on the seat of your bike where it can easily get knocked off; or on the handlebars or mirror, which can damage the inner liner. Always place it the right way up somewhere safe.

## Visors and Goggles

These are the essential attributes of visors and goggles.

### Eye Protection

Protecting the eyes is essential when riding a motorcycle. Visors or goggles protect your eyes from wind, rain, dust and insects.

### British Standard

Visors or goggles must display a BSI kite-mark showing compliance with BS4110 and be graded XA, YA or ZA. The letters denote the thickness of the glass or plastic, X being the thinnest and Z the thickest. The A denotes abrasion resistance.

### European Standard

Visors or goggles may comply with a European standard at least equivalent to BS4110 and display the relevant mark. Goggles may comply with the EU Directive on Personal Protective Equipment and carry the CE mark.

### Tinted Visors or Goggles

Legal tinted visors or goggles will display the BSI kite-mark and be clearly marked 'For Daytime Use Only'. Tinted eye protection should not be used in poor visibility. Heavily tinted or mirrored iridium visors are illegal for use on public roads.

### Cleaning

Visors and goggles should be kept clean and scratch free as dirt or scratches will impair your view and increase the dazzle of oncoming vehicle headlights or sunlight. Follow the manufacturer's advice for cleaning, and generally use only mild detergent and warm water, not abrasives or solvents.

## Protective Clothing

### Upper Body Protection

A custom-made motorcycle leather jacket will probably give the best protection; unstretched cowhide leather is very strong and resistant to abrasion. The jacket should be made of as few panels as possible, with good-quality double or triple stitching. The elbows, shoulders, back and kidneys should be protected by extra padding or armour. The zips and fastenings should be protected outside and inside, and the jacket should have stretch panels to allow movement around the shoulder area. Many jackets can be zipped to the leather trousers, which prevents the jacket from riding up over the shoulders in an accident and also keeps the back warm.

### One-piece Suits

Racing-style one-piece suits tend to be very expensive and are generally only used by the dedicated sports-bike enthusiast.

### Body Armour

There are many types of body armour on the market, ranging from kidney belts and back protectors to full body suits. If a manufacturer says the armour will protect you from injury, then it must comply with the EU Directive on Personal Protective Equipment and display the CE mark. Look out for the mark when making your purchase.

### Suitable Alternatives for Upper Body Protection

Other jackets specifically designed for motorcycling are made of very tough materials with many of the features of a good leather jacket and many have the added benefit of being waterproof. If nothing else is available then some form of heavy-duty work jacket will give some protection. Track suits or ski wear are not suitable for motorcycling as they give very little protection.

### Lower Body Protection

Leather trousers or jeans will probably give the best protection for the lower body. They should be well stitched with extra protection for the knees, hips and thighs, have a reinforced seat and protected zips and fastenings.

### Suitable Alternatives for Lower Body Protection

You can get trousers and jeans specifically designed for motorcycling and many of these are waterproof. If these are not an option, heavy denims will afford some protection. Only an idiot would wear shorts.

## Waterproofs

Leather is generally not waterproof and some sort of waterproof clothing is essential for a motorcyclist. Waterproofs should be specifically designed for motorcycling, and usually come as two-piece or one-piece suits.

## Footwear

Good-quality leather motorcycle boots will give the best protection as they have a good non-slip rubber sole and give support and protection for the heel, ankle and shin. They come in many different styles ranging from the lightweight sports boot to the heavy motocross boot. Many boots are not waterproof, but you can get waterproof inner liners or overboots. Whichever boots you choose, make sure you can comfortably operate the controls of the motorcycle when wearing them.

## Suitable Alternative Footwear

Army-style boots or Doc Martens™ will support and protect the heel and ankle. Flapping laces should be tucked away. Training shoes or wellington boots are not suitable for motorcycling as they give little protection.

## Gloves and Gauntlets

Hands and fingers should always be protected with good quality motorcycle gloves. Leather gloves give the required protection and are very supple. The gloves should be well stitched and have extra layers of leather on the palm and some protection for the fingers and the back of the hand. There should be some method of securing the glove around the wrist to prevent it coming off in an accident. Gloves come in all shapes and sizes, from lightweight summer gloves to heavy gauntlets and overmittens, but whichever you wear, make sure you can use the motorcycle controls safely.

## MODULE B:  Practical on-site training

This module will be covered outside on the off-road training area.

### THE CONTROLS OF THE MOTORCYCLE

Your instructor will introduce you to the motorcycle and show you around the controls so that by the end of this session you will know where all the controls are, what they do and how to operate them.

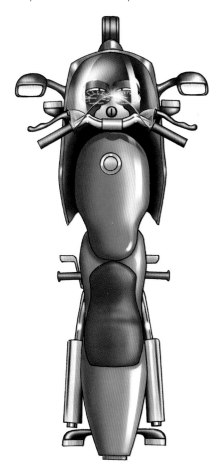

You will be shown and have explained to you the following controls.

### The Horn Button

The horn should not be used as a rebuke but only to warn people of your presence. It should not be used in a built-up area between 11.30 pm and 7.00 am or when stationary unless another moving vehicle poses a hazard.

### The Indicator Switch

This is generally located on the left handlebar. It may be a rocker switch or one that must be switched across each time. Some can be pushed to cancel, but most motorcycle indicators are not self-cancelling. Not cancelling the indicators is one of the more dangerous errors made by novice riders.

### The Light Switches

The location of these switches will vary depending on the motorcycle, but there will generally be a main switch and a separate high (full) and low-beam switch. High beam gives a wide spread of light but can dazzle other road users; a dipped headlight would normally be used unless travelling on unlit roads at night.

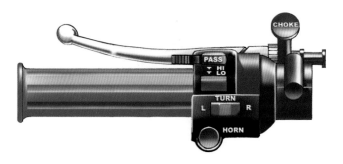

## The Instrument Panel

This will have a speedometer and amber or green warning lights for the indicators, plus the blue high-beam warning light. It may have a tachometer which lets you know how fast the engine is turning. A two-stroke machine will have a red oil warning light, and some machines have a temperature gauge. A green light indicates when the machine is in neutral (not in gear).

## The Ignition Switch and Steering Lock

A simple on-off switch operated by a key, sometimes including a position for parking lights and a steering lock. Most small motorcycles have a separate steering lock on the side of the frame headstock.

### The Engine Stop Switch

Some machines will have an emergency engine stop switch (sometimes called the 'kill switch') located on the right handlebar. This is for use in emergencies when the ignition switch cannot be reached. If you use it as the normal method for turning the engine off, you'll eventually leave your keys in the ignition.

### The Twist Grip Throttle

This is called the accelerator on a car. Twist it towards you and the engine goes faster, and so will the bike if it's in gear. Roll it away from you and the engine will slow to idling speed, and the bike will slow down. The throttle is usually fitted with a return spring and will automatically shut off if you let go of it.

### The Front Brake Lever

This is located on the right handlebar and should be operated with all four fingers of the right hand. If you use fewer, you'll trap the remaining fingers and not operate the brake properly.

### The Electric Starter Button

Most modern motorcycles have an electric starter. This is are located on the right handlebar and is operated with the right thumb. With the fuel and ignition on and with the machine out of gear, hold the starter button down until the engine fires. Some machines, particularly the new automatics, have both an electric starter and a kick-start lever.

### The Rear Brake Lever

On modern geared motorcycles, this is located next to the right footrest and should be operated by the right foot pivoting on the footrest. On automatics, it is on the left handlebar just like a pedal cycle and should be operated with all four fingers of the left hand. With most automatics, the rear brake must be applied before starting the engine.

### The Kick-start Lever

On most geared motorcycles, this is located on the right side of the machine near the footrest. On many new automatics, it is on the left towards the rear of the machine. With geared motorcycles, it is best to sit astride the machine to use the kick-start with the right foot, while supporting the weight of the bike with the left foot on the ground. With many automatics, it is best to start them on the stand.

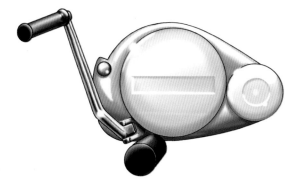

### The Fuel Tap

On most motorcycles, this is located under and to the side of the fuel tank. Larger machines and many modern automatics are fitted with a fuel gauge and do not have a manual fuel tap, instead fuel is fed on demand through a vacuum tap. Manual fuel taps have three standard positions: on, off and reserve. For normal running, the fuel tap should be in the on position. If the

fuel in the tank is allowed to reach a low level the engine will start to falter and the tap should be turned to the reserve position. When the machine is not in use the tap should be turned off.

### The Choke Lever

On most small motorcycles this is located on the side of the carburettor, and may have one or two positions. On some machines it will be on the left handlebar. Many automatics have automatic chokes. Using the choke reduces the air flowing into the carburettor and makes the fuel mixture richer, making cold-starting easier. The machine should be allowed to warm up on choke and the lever should then be returned to the off position before moving off.

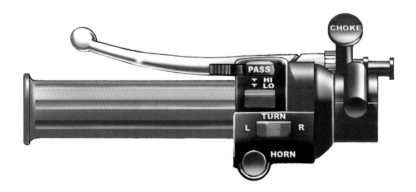

### The Gear Lever

This is located on the left side near the footrest and is operated by pivoting the left foot up and down on the footrest.

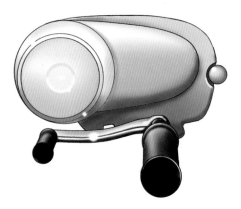

Some scooters have a twist-grip gear change on the left handlebar.

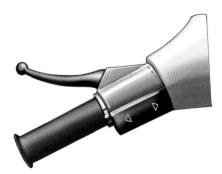

Most modern machines have four or five gears, but some have as many as seven. The gears are sequential, so each gear must be selected up and down the gearbox: for instance, you cannot go from first to third without passing through second on the way. The gear lever is spring-loaded and will return to the same resting position between gear changes. Neutral is between first and second gears.

### *The Clutch Lever*

This is located on the left handlebar and operates the clutch, which transfers the engine power to the rear wheel. Operate the lever with all four fingers for the best control. With the machine in gear and the lever pulled in to the handlebar, there is no drive to the rear wheel. As the lever is released, engine power is gradually transferred to the rear wheel and the machine begins to move. With the lever fully released, the engine power is linked directly to the rear wheel. When used properly in conjunction with the throttle, the clutch allows smooth moving off and gear-changing, and allows the machine to come to a halt without stalling the engine.

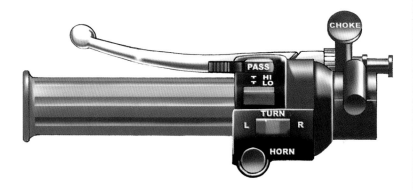

## USING THE CENTRE STAND AND SIDE STAND

Some machines come with both stands and some with just one. Your instructor should explain how to use them properly and demonstrate how to use them before allowing you to practise.

Many learners have problems taking motorcycles off and putting them on the centre stand, and doing so safely requires technique rather than brute strength. With practice, almost anyone can do it.

Motorcycles should only be parked on firm ground. If the stand sinks into the ground, the machine will fall over and could injure someone. If you have no choice, place something under the stand to help spread the weight. A small block of wood, a flat stone or brick, even a flattened drinks can will suffice; put the stand in the centre of whatever you use, otherwise it may tip up under the weight of the motorcycle.

Motorcycle stands are designed to take the weight of the machine and not the rider. If you sit on a motorcycle when it is on a stand you risk damaging the stand – and they're not cheap!

Side stand                                    Centre stand

### Taking the Motorcycle Off the Centre Stand

Because we ride on the left in Britain, it is safer to mount and dismount the motorcycle from the left.

1. Stand to the left, facing the side of the machine with your feet slightly apart for best balance.

2. Make sure the front wheel is facing forwards, and with your left hand grip the left handlebar. With your right hand, grip somewhere solid to the rear of the machine; most bikes have a grab handle or rail specifically designed for the job.

3. Rest just the toes of your right foot on the centre-stand lever.

4. Gently rock the machine backwards, then pull it forwards off the stand.

5. As the machine rolls off the stand, apply gentle pressure to the centre-stand lever, keeping it in contact with the ground. This stops the machine rolling away until you can apply the front brake.

6. Lean the machine towards you a little and it will be easy to transfer your right hand to the front brake.

7. Once the front brake is applied you can flick the stand up, and either wheel the machine or sit astride it.

### *Placing the Motorcycle On the Centre Stand*

1. Standing to the left as before, hold the handlebars and keep the front brake applied.

2. Use your right foot on the centre-stand lever to bring the centre stand down and into contact with the ground.

3. Lean the machine slightly away from you and make sure both legs of the stand touch the ground.

4. Release the front brake and take hold of somewhere solid at the rear of the machine, preferably a grab rail.

5. Place the ball of your right foot on the centre-stand lever, bend your right knee and press firmly down on the lever. At the same time lift the back of the machine and it will roll backwards on to its stand.

### Taking the Motorcycle Off the Side Stand

Setting off with the side stand down can be at best embarrassing, and at worst fatal! Make sure the side stand is fully retracted before getting on the machine. Some side stands are fitted with cut-out switches or strong springs to prevent you riding off with the stand down.

1. Lean over from the left, take hold of the handlebars and apply the front brake.

2. Lean the machine slightly away from you and use your right foot to retract the side stand.

## *Placing the Motorcycle On the Side Stand*

1. Dismount on the left, holding the handlebars and keeping the front brake applied.

2. Use your right foot to extend the side stand fully.

3. Lean the machine over until it is supported by the stand, and pull it backwards a little to make sure it is firmly located on the stand.

4. Turn the front wheel to the left to reduce the chance of the bike rolling off the stand.

If you are forced to park facing downhill, wedge the front wheel in against the kerb and leave the machine in gear.

## CHECKING YOUR MOTORCYCLE

Your instructor will explain, and if necessary demonstrate, the important safety checks you will need to do in order to maintain a safe, roadworthy motorcycle.

### *Daily Checks*

You will be shown how to conduct the following daily checks.

#### *Petrol and Oil*
Your oil should be at the correct level and you should have sufficient fuel for your journey.

#### *Brakes*
Test both brakes to make sure they work properly.

#### *Tyres*
Make sure both tyres are correctly inflated.

#### *Electrics*
Test your lights, brake lights, indicators and horn.

#### *Mirrors*
Make sure the mirrors are clean, secure and properly adjusted.

### *Weekly Checks*

Most motorcycles come with an owner's handbook. If you have one, follow the manufacturer's advice when it comes to weekly checks. If you don't have one, at least once a week take a walk around the bike and conduct the following checks. Your instructor will show you how to do them.

### Cables and Hydraulic Hoses

Check all cable-operated controls such as the front brake, clutch and throttle. Check the inner and outer cables for fraying or damage; the cable should move smoothly, be properly adjusted and well lubricated. If the machine has hydraulic brakes or clutch, check the hoses and connections for damage or leakage and check the level of hydraulic fluid in the reservoir.

### Suspension

Check the front and rear suspension systems for leakage and corrosion, and make sure the settings are correct.

### Wheels and Tyres

Check your tyres for wear and damage. The minimum tread depth for motorcycle tyres is 1 mm; for mopeds it's visible tread. The tread pattern must cover at least three-quarters of the width of the tyre for the whole circumference and include the centre section. Follow the manufacturer's recommendations and check the tyre pressures with the tyres cold. Check the wheel rims and spokes for damage; problems with wheels should be fixed by a wheel builder.

### Oil

Turn off the engine and place the bike on its centre stand on level ground (if you only have a side stand, get someone to hold the bike upright). Allow time for the oil to drain into the sump, then check the engine oil level. If you have a two-stroke machine you will need to check the two-stroke oil reservoir.

### Brakes

Check discs, drums, pads and shoes for wear, and make sure any levers and cables are properly adjusted.

### Drive Chain

Make sure the chain is properly adjusted and well lubricated; the free play should be within the manufacturer's recommendations and is usually measured halfway along the bottom run of the chain.

### Battery

This is usually located somewhere under the seat. Check that the terminals are clean and secure. Check the electrolyte level, and if necessary top up with distilled water.

### Cooling System

With air-cooled machines, check the fins on the cylinder for damage and clogging. With liquid-cooled machines, check the system for leaks and make sure the expansion chamber is topped up with the correct coolant.

### Cleaning and Lubrication

A clean machine looks good and holds its value. As you wash the machine, check for any loose nuts or bolts. Avoid pressure washers as these get water in the bearings and other areas and may cause damage. After washing, re-lubricate the levers, cables and chain and anywhere else that may need it.

## WHEELING THE MOTORCYCLE

Your instructor will explain and demonstrate how to wheel your machine to the left and right under control, with proper balance, bringing it to a safe halt using the front brake.

When you practise make sure you:

* Take the machine off the stand correctly.

* Lean the machine slightly towards you for better balance.

- Stand so your right thigh is roughly where the tank meets the seat.

- Be careful not to clip your right shin on the footrest as you walk.

- Keep your right hand over the front brake lever and if necessary apply it gently with all four fingers.

- Only use the brake when the machine is upright and straight.

- Look where you are going.

## STARTING AND STOPPING THE ENGINE

At last you can begin to learn to ride the bike! Your instructor will explain and demonstrate how to safely start and stop the engine before allowing you to practise. There are two useful acronyms to remember for starting the engine.

If you are using a geared motorcycle, remember **FIGS**.

- **F** is for fuel: make sure the fuel is on and if necessary use the choke.

- **I** is for ignition: turn the key to the on position.

- **G** is for green light: make sure the gearshift is in neutral.

- **S** is for start: use the electric or kick-starter until the engine starts.

If you are using an automatic, remember **FIBS**.

- **F** is for fuel.

- **I** is for ignition.

- **B** is for brake: apply the rear brake before starting.

- **S** is for start.

Now you're ready to move on to the next module, practical on-site riding.

## MODULE C:  Practical on-site riding

This section will be covered on an approved off-road training area.

### MOVING OFF AND STOPPING

Your instructor will explain in detail how to move off and stop safely in a straight line. Then the procedure will be demonstrated step by step so you can see exactly what is needed. Make sure you watch carefully, as before you get to practise you must know:

- What to do.

- How to do it.

- Where to go.

- Where to stop.

- How to stop.

### How to Move Off on a Geared Motorcycle

1. Take the machine off the stand and sit astride it.

2. Keep the front brake applied, and start the engine.

3. Pull the clutch in and select first gear.

4. Apply the rear brake and release the front brake.

5. Set the throttle slightly busier than tick-over.

6. Slowly release the clutch to the biting point; the engine note will change.

7. Release the rear brake.

8. Gently increase the throttle as you slowly release the clutch all the way.

## *How to Move Off on an Automatic Motorcycle*

1. Release the rear brake.

2. Twist the throttle and go!

### *Points to Remember*

Now you are moving, make sure that:

- You look where you're going, not at the instrument panel!

- You put your feet on the footrests and grip the tank with your knees.

- You sit comfortably on the rider's seat with your elbows slightly bent.

- You hold the handlebars properly, not covering the brake or clutch levers.

### *Braking*

A motorcycle has two brakes. The front brake is the most effective because when it is applied, the weight of the rider and the motorcycle is pitched forwards on to the front tyre. The tyre spreads out, thereby gaining more grip on the road surface.

For the best effect, the front brake is normally applied just before the rear. All braking should be done with the machine upright and travelling in a straight line. It can be dangerous to use the brakes when turning, or with the machine banked (leaned) over.

## How to Stop Safely

If you think ABC you won't go far wrong!

- **A** is for accelerator (throttle) off.

- **B** is for brakes on, gently.

- **C** is for clutch in, so as not to stall the engine.

## Other Important Elements

While you practise this basic moving off and stopping exercise, your instructor will introduce the following elements.

### Safety Position

Whenever the bike is stationary you should have a brake applied. By doing so you show a brake light to the rear and hopefully this will prevent anyone from running into the back of you. The rear brake is the best one to use because you then have your right hand free to control the throttle, and if someone does run into the back of you, the machine is less likely to tip you over the handlebars.

### Blind Spots

Blind spots are the areas to the left and right and immediately behind you that are not covered by the mirrors.

### Lifesaver Observations

A lifesaver look is a final glance into the appropriate blind spot before moving position or turning. It is particularly relevant in busy traffic when turning left or right, but may not be required when travelling at higher speed on quieter roads when you're certain what's going on behind you.

### Rear Observations

Effective rear observations using the mirrors and looking over your shoulder are essential for safe riding. Allowing your eyes to focus will allow you time to assess the speed and distance of following traffic. A rear observation should be made by turning the head, not by twisting from the waist, which can affect your stability.

Good rear observations should be made before:

- Moving off or stopping.

- Accelerating or slowing down.

- Turning left or right.

- Moving position, changing lanes or overtaking.

It is possible to look behind at the wrong time. Work on achieving a good balance of rear observations over your shoulder and using the mirrors.

### Common Faults During Moving Off and Stopping

- Poor clutch control: releasing the lever too quickly and stalling the engine.

- Poor throttle control: setting the throttle too high or too low.

- Not releasing the rear brake, thereby stalling the engine.

- Not looking ahead: looking at the front wheel or instrument panel.

- Riding position: sitting on the pillion seat, not gripping the tank.

- Braking too much or too little when stopping.

- Safety position: not keeping the rear brake applied when stationary.

- Poor observations: too many, too few, too long or too short.

### Achievements

By the end of this session you should be able to:

- Move off smoothly without stalling.

- Stop safely and under control.

- Make effective rear observations when necessary.

## GEAR CHANGING

Your instructor will explain and demonstrate gear changing in detail.

Gears allow you to go faster for the same amount of effort from the engine – very similar to a pedal cycle except that on a pedal cycle you're the engine!

### When to Change Gear

Listen to the engine tone. Experience will tell you when to change up or down the gearbox. Essentially you should change before the engine is:

- Racing or stressed in too low a gear.

- Labouring or chugging along in too high a gear.

### How to Change Gear

1. Place your foot either under or over the gear lever in preparation.

2. Simultaneously close the throttle and pull in the clutch.

3. Change gear.

4. Smoothly release the clutch.

5. Open the throttle gently and take up the drive in the new gear.

Note:

- When changing down gear it may be necessary to slow down first using the throttle and brakes.

- When stopping at junctions, slow down in second gear and select first gear just as you stop. This allows you to move away quickly if required.

### Common Faults in Gear Changing

- Looking down: always look ahead and feel for the lever with your foot.

- Throttle: not closing the throttle prior to changing gear, or opening it too soon after gear changing.

- Clutch: pulling it in too early or releasing it too quickly.

- Wrong gear: moving the gear lever more than once or in the wrong direction.

### Achievements

By the end of this session you should be able to:

- Change smoothly up and down the gearbox.

- Match the gear to your speed.

## SLOW CONTROL

Your instructor will now explain and demonstrate how to travel slowly on a motorcycle before allowing you to practise various exercises. It is essential to master this skill as you need to be smooth and in control of the machine at all times. Travelling in first gear and trying to control your speed just using the throttle is very difficult and can affect your balance.

### When to Use Slow Control

In today's busy traffic there are many situations when you will need to travel slowly and smoothly with your feet on the footrests, for example:

- In queues of slow-moving traffic.

- When turning left or right at narrow junctions.

- When doing a U-turn in the road.

## *How to Attain Slow Control*

To travel slowly in first gear at walking pace you need to achieve a good balance of the following controls:

- The throttle: keep it slightly open to maintain drive and avoid stalling.

- The clutch: keep it just at the biting point, not too far in or out.

- The rear brake: it provides adequate braking when travelling slowly, so use it gently to control your speed.

When you have practised travelling slowly in a straight line your instructor will ask you to practise some further exercises, including the following:

- A figure of eight: make sure you don't turn too tightly to start off.

- A U-turn: make sure you look both ways first and control the clutch.

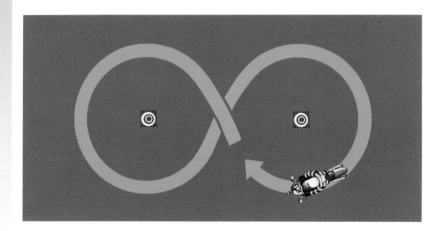

### Common Faults during Slow Control

- Poor throttle control: setting the throttle too high or too low.

- Poor clutch control: pulling the clutch too far in or letting it out too far.

- Rear brake: not using the brake or using it too much.

### Achievements

By the end of this session you should be able to:

- Travel safely and smoothly at a walking pace.

- Be able to vary your speed when necessary.

- Turn left and right slowly and smoothly.

- Complete a figure of eight without putting your feet down.

- Complete a safe U-turn with good observations, keeping your feet on the footrests.

## THE EMERGENCY STOP

Before riding on the road you will be expected to show that you can bring your motorcycle to a safe controlled stop as if in an emergency. Before practising, your instructor will explain the exercise and demonstrate the procedure.

### Stopping Quickly and Safely

If something unexpected happens, causing you to stop quickly, you should:

1. Close off the throttle to lose the drive from the engine.

2. Squeeze the front brake: remember it's the most effective brake.

3. Use the rear brake: this stabilises the machine and slows the bike further.

4. Continue squeezing the front brake: slowing down quickly and safely.

5. Pull in the clutch just before the engine stalls.

Changing gear as you do an emergency stop is generally not recommended. To change down gears, the clutch will disengage, disconnecting the drive to the rear wheel and increasing the chances of it locking up.

If you change gear in the final phases of the emergency stop you will be tempted to put your right foot down as you stop. Avoid doing so as you will be letting go of the rear brake.

## Wet or Poor Road Surfaces

If the road surface is wet or poor it will take at least twice as long to stop. To avoid locking up the wheels or skidding, apply the front brake less heavily than you would on a dry, firm surface.

## Skid Control

The best skid control is not to get into one in the first place; good observation of the road surface and sensible use of the brakes will reduce the risk.

The main causes of skidding are:

- Late harsh braking.

- Violent acceleration (wheel spin).

- Erratic changes of direction.

- Leaning the motorcycle over too far.

### How to Control a Front Wheel Skid

1. Release the front brake, allowing the front wheel to rotate.

2. Reapply the front brake more gently.

### How to Control a Rear Wheel Skid

1. Release the rear brake.

2. If the rear wheel has swerved out to the left or right, steer in that direction.

3. Get the machine travelling straight.

4. Reapply the rear brake more gently.

## Common Faults during Emergency Stops

- Throttle: not closing the throttle or pinching it as you apply the front brake.

- Brakes: braking too much or too little or only using one brake.

- Clutch: pulling it in too early, causing the rear wheel to lock up and skid.

- Changing gear: putting the right foot down and releasing the rear brake.

## LEFT AND RIGHT TURNS

You will be required to practise simulated left and right turns on the training area. The area will have junctions marked out on it or your instructor may lay out cones to simulate junctions. Your instructor will explain the correct system and demonstrate it for you.

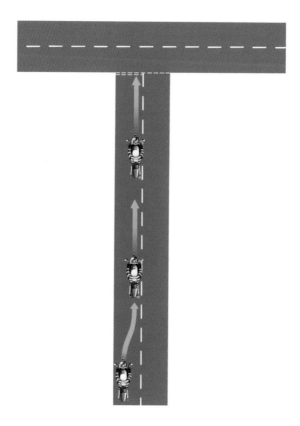

## OSM-PSL

Here's another sequence for you to remember. You will be expected to use the OSM-PSL system for turning left and right.

- **O**bservation: use the mirrors and when necessary a rear observation.

- **S**ignal: use the indicators or an arm signal to inform others.

- **M**anoeuvre: get yourself into the correct position.

- **P**osition: approach the turn from the correct road position.

- **S**peed: reduce speed as necessary using the throttle, brakes and gears.

- **L**ook: thoroughly check the road on to which you are turning.

### Assessing the Junction

On the approach to a junction you will need to check the signs and road markings. At some junctions you are required to give way, while at others you must stop and give way. Some junctions are unmarked and these must be treated with great caution.

## Turning Left from a Minor Road into a Major Road

1. **O**bserve, use your mirrors and make a rear observation if appropriate.

2. **S**ignal left in plenty of time on the approach.

3. **M**anoeuvre to the correct position.

4. **P**osition to the left but away from the gutter.

5. **S**peed adjustment: slow down and be prepared to give way or stop.

6. **L**ook in all directions at the earliest opportunity; remember, the first danger usually comes from the right. Observations to the right, left and right would normally be the minimum, and they should be good focused looks.

## Turning Right from a Minor Road into a Major Road

1. **O**bserve, use your mirrors and make a rear observation if appropriate.

2. **S**ignal right in plenty of time on the approach.

3. **M**anoeuvre to the correct position in plenty of time.

4. **P**osition to the right of your lane if it is safe; avoid riding on any white lines and don't stray into the opposite lane.

5. **S**peed adjustment: slow down and be prepared to stop or give way.

6. **L**ook in all directions at the earliest opportunity; remember, the first danger usually comes from the right. Observations to the right, left and right would normally be the minimum, and they should be good focused looks.

   Watch for vehicles approaching from your left and indicating to turn right into the minor road as they may cut the corner. You might have to give way earlier than usual.

7. Take a lifesaver look over your right shoulder before turning. Make sure you do this early enough to take any avoiding action that might be needed.

8. Without cutting the corner, turn into the left-hand lane. Cutting the corner will cause you to turn into the face of opposing traffic.

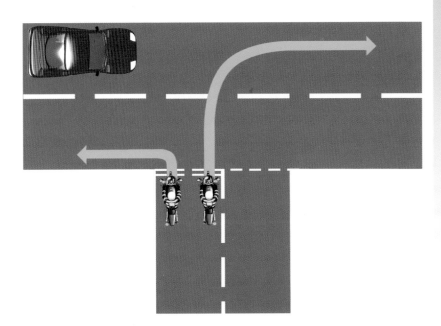

## *Turning Left from a Major Road into a Minor Road*

As you approach the junction, look for pedestrians who are crossing or waiting to cross. If someone is crossing the mouth of the junction you should give way to them. Be especially wary of children and be prepared to use your horn to warn people of your presence.

1. **O**bserve, use your mirrors and make a rear observation if appropriate.

2. **S**ignal left in plenty of time on the approach.

3. **M**anoeuvre to the correct position.

4. **P**osition slightly to the left, well away from the gutter.

5. **S**peed adjustment: slow down to suit the turn.

6. **L**ook into the junction, watching for pedestrians who may not have seen you. Take special care when crossing bus or cycle lanes. A lifesaver look over your left shoulder may be necessary to watch out for pedal cyclists or other motorcyclists coming up on your left.

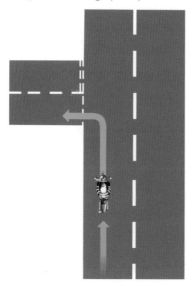

## *Turning Right from a Major Road into a Minor Road*

1. **O**bserve, use the mirrors and make a rear observation if appropriate.

2. **S**ignal right in plenty of time on the approach.

3. **M**anoeuvre to the correct position.

4. **P**osition to the right of your lane if it's safe; avoid riding on any white lines and don't stray into the opposite lane.

5. **S**peed adjustment: slow down and be prepared to give way to oncoming traffic.

6. **L**ook into the junction; watch for pedestrians who may be crossing and vehicles turning out of the junction that may cut across your path.

7. If you have to give way to oncoming traffic before turning, stop halfway across the mouth of the junction into which you're turning. This will make it easier to turn without cutting the corner.

8. Take a lifesaver look before turning, watching out for vehicles overtaking to your right. Make sure you do this in time to take any avoiding action.

## Obstructed View at Junctions

Very often objects such as parked vehicles, hedges or trees will obstruct your view into a junction. Slow down and be prepared to stop. If necessary, edge forwards until you get a good view, and check it's safe before continuing.

## Clutch Control at Junctions

When turning at narrow junctions, good clutch control is essential. When turning left, poor clutch control will cause you to swing wide towards the opposite side of the road. When turning right, it will cause you to swing wide towards the gutter or pavement.

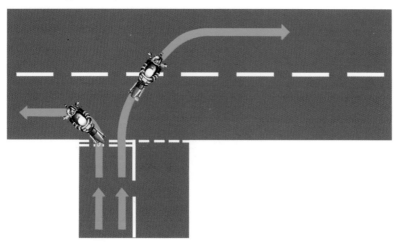

### Misleading Signals

It's important not to signal too early, especially when junctions are close together. The system can be adapted so the signal is given a little later, so as not to mislead other road users.

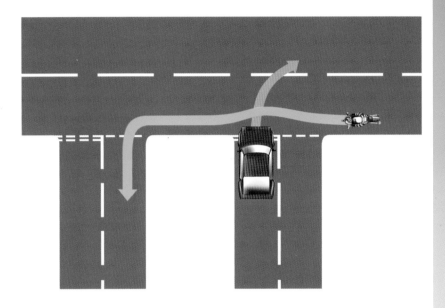

### After Completing a Turn

Having completed a turn you should:

1. Cancel your signal.

2. Use your mirrors to check the situation behind you.

3. Take up the correct road position for the conditions, and accelerate briskly and smoothly to a suitable speed within the given speed limit.

## *Common Faults during Left and Right Turns*

- Observations: Over the wrong shoulder, in the wrong direction or not at all.

- Signals: Signalling too late or too early or not at all, or failing to cancel indicators after turning.

- Manoeuvre: Moving before observing or signalling or moving too late.

- Position: Positioning too close or too far to the left or right.

- Speed: Slowing down too early or approaching too fast.

- Look: Looking too often or not often enough; not allowing time for the eyes to focus.

- Clutch: Poor clutch control, leading to loss of control.

## MODULE D: Practical on-road training

This section will normally be covered in a classroom out of any inclement weather – and hopefully well equipped with refreshment and toilet facilities. Your instructor will give you a detailed pre-ride briefing, covering the following subjects.

### LEGAL REQUIREMENTS FOR RIDING ON THE ROAD

- You must have reached at least the minimum age for the machine you are riding (see pages 35 and 36).

- You must have a valid licence with the correct entitlement, and this must be signed.

- You must wear an approved motorcycle safety helmet, which must be properly fastened.

- You must display L-plates (D-plates may be used in Wales).

- You must have a valid certificate of insurance or cover note.

- You must have a valid MOT certificate if your machine is more than three years old.

- Your machine must be legal, safe and roadworthy.

- You must correctly display a valid Vehicle Excise Licence.

## WHY MOTORCYCLISTS ARE VULNERABLE

- Because of the size of their vehicle (particularly the width), motorcyclists are not easily seen.

- Motorcyclists are easily hidden from view by parked vehicles, hedges, lamp posts and other objects.

- Motorcyclists have to balance and have less contact with the road surface than other road users.

- Motorcyclists are affected by crosswinds and buffeting on windy days.

- Motorcyclists can be affected by air turbulence caused by other vehicles.

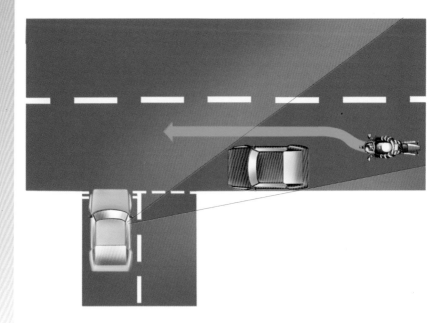

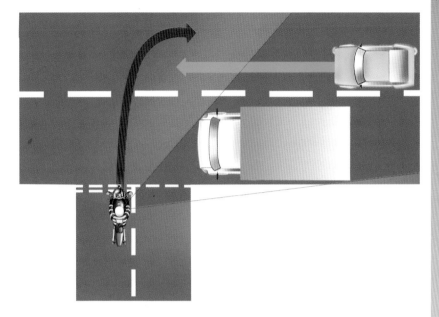

## THE IMPORTANCE OF BEING CLEARLY VISIBLE

Fluorescent or dayglo clothing and equipment will make you more visible during daylight hours. Reflective clothing and equipment is needed for night-time.

Your helmet is often the first thing seen by other road users, so choose one that will stand out in all weathers. A white one is most easily spotted, day or night. Other brightly-coloured helmets are all right for daytime use, but often appear much darker under orange sodium street lights.

Riding with a dipped headlight during the day can make you more visible, particularly on a dull day. It may not be wise on a bumpy road surface, however, because the headlight could appear to be flashing. If the sun is behind you, then using a headlight may do more to obscure the motorcycle.

## THE IMPORTANCE OF CORRECT POSITIONING

When riding on a road with no hazards it is best to position near the centre of the lane. By riding here you are more visible and you have a good view of the road.

If you ride in the gutter you won't be very visible; you'll be riding in loose dirt and debris and other road users are likely to drive alongside you.

If you ride too far over to the right you will be in danger from the oncoming traffic, particularly those encroaching on to your lane as they overtake parked vehicles.

In heavily congested urban areas, deposits of oil dropped from other vehicles can build up in the centre of the lane. This can be very slippery, particularly in wet weather. If necessary, position yourself just to the left of this grease line.

Be flexible with your riding position, adapting it to best suit the situation.

Position correctly for left and right turns at junctions and crossroads. When travelling straight on at crossroads, traffic lights and pedestrian crossings it is best to ride in the centre of your lane. This dominant position is also the best one to use when travelling in a dedicated lane.

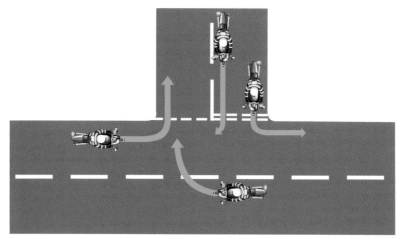

Positioning on the approach to roundabouts is similar to that used when turning at junctions and crossroads. While travelling around the island you should position to the left when turning left or going straight on, and to the right when turning right.

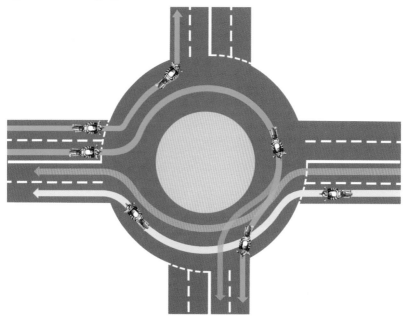

Where there are junctions or driveways to the left, it may be sensible to position to the right of your lane to be more easily seen and to gain a better view. Do this only if oncoming traffic allows and it's safe.

When overtaking parked vehicles, leave at least a door's width between you and the vehicle. Remember a lorry's door is wider than a car's!

When overtaking a moving vehicle, position well away so as not to be affected by the air turbulence.

## THE IMPORTANCE OF GOOD REAR OBSERVATION

Mirrors should be used regularly to check the conditions behind. Remember that mirrors have big blind spots that will need to be checked. Some mirrors give a distorted view, and if they vibrate the image will be blurred. Using mirrors alone makes it difficult to judge speed and distance.

Turning your head to look behind makes it easier to judge the speed and distance of other vehicles.

You must make effective rear observations before moving off, stopping, accelerating, slowing down, moving position or turning.

A lifesaver look is a final glance into the appropriate blind spot before moving position or turning.

You must use the lifesaver at the right time. The consequences of looking behind at the wrong moment could be disastrous.

## THE IMPORTANCE OF KEEPING A SAFE DISTANCE

It's difficult to judge how long a yard, a metre or a car length is; everyone has their own idea. Using a time gap makes things much easier because we can all count seconds quite easily. We use the 'two-second rule'.

On a good, dry road surface, a two-second gap between you and the vehicle in front will give a safe overall stopping distance at all speeds. The size of the gap will increase as the speed increases. As the vehicle in front passes a stationary object such as a lamp post, start to count to two seconds. You should have finished your count by the time you reach that same stationary object. Now you have a two-second gap.

Saying 'Only a fool breaks the two-second rule' takes about two seconds.

If the road surface is poor or wet, it will take at least twice as long to stop, so you should use a gap of at least four seconds.

Keeping a safe distance away from traffic means you have a far better view of the road surface and the traffic conditions ahead. Because you have a better view, you have much more time to react.

Keeping a good distance behind large vehicles means the drivers of those vehicles can see you in their mirrors.

# KNOW THE EFFECTS OF VARIOUS WEATHER CONDITIONS
## Sunlight

Sunlight can dazzle you, in which case an approved tinted visor or sunglasses may be useful. When the sun is low and behind you it can dazzle other road users and they may not see the motorcycle. It can shine directly on the indicators or brake light, making it difficult for other road users to see them. Sunlight reflected on a wet road surface can be very dangerous.

## Wet Conditions

In wet weather you must slow down and increase your distance from other vehicles. Being wet and miserable will affect your concentration, so make sure you're well prepared with a good set of waterproofs.

## Wind

On a windy day expect to be blown about a little. Be careful on exposed roads or at junctions and crossroads in urban areas. You can lean into a side wind to compensate and maintain your position, but if you enter a sheltered area remember to sit up. Overtaking large vehicles on a windy day can be particularly difficult and hazardous.

## Fog

If it's foggy or misty follow the 'Fog Code'. Consider whether your journey is necessary and, if not, don't travel. If you must travel, use dipped headlights; if visibility is less than 100 metres also use fog lights (if fitted); slow down and increase your gap, don't 'tailgate' by riding too close to the vehicle in front; keep your visor clear. Remember, fog and mist can be patchy; one minute it can be bright and sunny, the next you can't see your hand in front of your face!

### Snow and Ice

If it's snowing it would be sensible not to ride a motorcycle. If it's unavoidable, try to use main roads as they are more likely to have been salted. Remember snow will cover road signs and markings and you must take great care at junctions and other hazards.

If it's icy, try to avoid riding. Remember, even on a sunny day in winter, frost and ice can linger in shaded areas under trees, hedges and bridges. If the road surface appears to be wet and you can't hear any sound from your tyres, you may be riding on black ice.

## KNOW THE EFFECTS OF VARIOUS ROAD SURFACES
### Fuel and Oil

Spilt fuel and oil is a common hazard on today's busy roads. Diesel fuel is particularly dangerous for the motorcyclist because it remains on the road far longer than other fuels, which evaporate more quickly. Wet roads make these spills even more dangerous. Fuel and oil have a multicoloured appearance when mixed with water. Watch for diesel and oil on bends and at roundabouts, bus stops, taxi ranks and service stations. Try to avoid riding on any spillage, but if it's unavoidable keep the motorcycle upright and take great care.

## Gravel and Debris

Loose gravel and debris collects in the gutters and other disused areas of the road, on roundabouts and in the centre of busy junctions. Avoid riding over these areas as the loose surface will reduce tyre grip and increase the risk of skidding. If it's unavoidable reduce your speed, keep the motorcycle upright and be very careful. On newly surfaced roads reduce your speed, increase your safe gap and use your visor or goggles to protect your eyes from flying stone chips.

## Manhole Covers and Uneven Road Surfaces

Metal manhole covers and inspection hatches can be very slippery, particularly when wet, and they are very often positioned on your riding line. Try to avoid riding over them, but do not swerve erratically to do so; if it's unavoidable be careful and keep the machine upright.

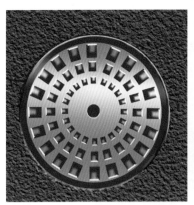 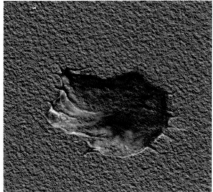

Watch out for potholes and rutted road surfaces; try to spot them early enough and avoid swerving over them.

### Road Markings

The paint used for road markings contains microscopic glass granules to aid reflectivity and this is very slippery when wet. When possible, avoid braking or leaning the bike over on this paint as it greatly reduces tyre grip.

### Road Repairs

Tar over banding is used to seal around road repairs. This is very slippery in the wet; avoid braking or leaning the machine over on it as it reduces tyre grip.

### Wet Leaves

Wet leaves in autumn reduce to slippery mush and should be avoided.

## RIDING AT THE CORRECT SPEED FOR THE ROAD AND TRAFFIC CONDITIONS

When the road surface is wet or poor, you should reduce your speed accordingly and increase your gap. You become vulnerable if you ride too quickly for the conditions. Riding at 30 miles per hour along a busy road with cars parked on both sides may not be safe.

The faster you go, the more you concentrate on what's happening in the distance, so your side vision becomes less effective. You might not spot the child about to run out into the road or the car emerging from the driveway, and you'll have less time to react. Your side or peripheral vision is very sensitive to movement. Once a movement is detected, it cues your central vision to look at it. Slowing down improves your chances of spotting and avoiding hazards.

You can be vulnerable if you travel too slowly for the conditions and fail to keep up with the traffic flow. Other drivers will become impatient and try to edge you into the gutter or intimidate you by driving very close behind. However, you must never exceed the set speed limit, even to keep up with a flow of traffic.

They say 'speed kills'. While riding fast may not kill you, not being able to stop in time certainly will.

## KNOW THE IMPORTANCE OF HAZARD PERCEPTION

You must work hard to perfect your observational skills and spot all the hazards on today's roads. A hazard can be created by the movement of other road users, by obstructions such as parked vehicles and street furniture, by the weather, or by physical features such as a bend or hill crest, the road layout or surface.

You must constantly assess and reassess the conditions; if you fail to spot a hazard the results can be unfortunate.

## KNOW HOW TO RIDE DEFENSIVELY AND ANTICIPATE THE ACTIONS OF OTHERS

Good concentration helps anticipation, and if you can anticipate the actions of others you will ride safely and defensively.

Don't rely on the signals of others; they may have forgotten to cancel them. This is particularly important when someone is indicating to turn left into a junction you are exiting. Always expect the unexpected and trust no one.

Look for the clues. If people are getting up from their seats on a bus, then the bus will probably stop at the bus stop and you may need to slow down or change your position. If a ball bounces out into the road, slow down and start looking for the child who is likely to follow.

## KNOW THE CONSEQUENCES OF AGGRESSIVE ATTITUDES WHEN RIDING

The popular term for aggression when driving is 'road rage'. If you lose your temper with someone you will concentrate on that person to the exclusion of all other hazards, and by doing so you are more likely to be involved in an accident. Retaliating by riding erratically or too close to the vehicle in front only puts you at risk and is foolish.

Remember, nobody's perfect: we all make mistakes. Try to be courteous and understanding. If someone really upsets you, then you should stop and calm down before continuing your journey.

## KNOW THE EFFECTS OF ALCOHOL, DRUGS, FATIGUE AND ILLNESS

Drinking and riding will lengthen your reaction time, impair your judgement of speed and distance and affect your balance and concentration. Even a small amount of alcohol in your bloodstream will affect your reaction times. The only advice is not to drink and ride.

The legal limit is 80 mg/100 ml alcohol to blood. Remember it's possible to be over this limit the morning after.

Prohibited drugs will have similar effects as alcohol. Even prescription or patent medicines from your pharmacist can have undesirable effects such as drowsiness and many warn against operating heavy machinery. A motorcycle is heavy machinery: if in doubt don't ride.

If you're very tired or ill, your concentration and judgement will be adversely affected, so don't ride a motorcycle.

## THE IMPORTANCE OF UNDERSTANDING THE HIGHWAY CODE

*The Highway Code* (HMSO, £1.49) is a rule book for what can essentially be a dangerous game. To survive, you need to know the rules and adhere to them. Knowing the Highway Code will reduce the chances of you being involved in an accident, so you should read and understand all the rules in the current edition.

The list of signs and markings in the Highway Code booklet is not a comprehensive one, so make sure you are familiar with all the traffic signs and road markings by reading *Know Your Traffic Signs* (HMSO, £2.50).

# MODULE E: Practical on-road riding

This is when everything you've learnt and practised should pay off. For this final module you will be out on the public roads with your instructor, proving that you can ride to a basic, safe standard. It can be nerve-wracking to begin with but try to relax. As long as you listen to your instructor you will be safe.

When on the public roads you and your instructor must comply with certain regulations:

- By law, there must be no more than two students per instructor.

- You must spend at least two hours on the road.

- Your motorcycles must be roadworthy and legal.

- You must be in radio contact.

- You must wear fluorescent or reflective clothing.

Your on-road training will cover how to deal safely with many hazards and road conditions, including the following:

- Many types of junctions.

- Roundabouts.

- Traffic lights and pedestrian crossings.

- Bends and obstructions.

- Gradients (hills).

Initially your instructor will guide you with step-by-step instructions over the radio. As you become more confident, the instructions will gradually reduce to simple route direction, and you will be expected to show that you can do everything else for yourself. You will stop occasionally and your instructor will talk about your ride. Listen carefully and work at improving any points raised.

When you have satisfactorily completed this module, your instructor will issue you with a Certificate of Completion (DL196). This certificate validates your provisional motorcycle entitlement and licenses you to ride on public roads as a learner. You must still display L-plates and you cannot carry a pillion passenger. Now you need to concentrate on further practice before taking your moped or motorcycle test. Remember, CBT is only *basic* training, so ask your instructor about further training.

Once you have completed your CBT, you have two options open to you: you can book further training, or you can practise by yourself before taking the test. Let's face it, there are few learners who pass the test without taking further training. Why waste your test fee and time on a test you probably won't pass?

## THE THEORY TEST

All provisional licence holders must sit and pass the theory test before booking a practical test. If you hold a full car licence and are riding on the provisional motorcycle entitlement, you are currently exempt from taking the theory test, although there's legislation in the pipeline to change this. Your training body or local DSA test centre will be able to supply you with details of your local theory test centre and how to book a test.

You need to prepare properly for the test, so ask your instructor for some sample test papers and study the Highway Code thoroughly. The test questions have multiple-choice answers and deal with matters ranging from road signs to general vehicle maintenance. This test is now computer-based, using touch-screen monitors which provide same-day results.

This is one exam where you can legally buy the answers. There are a number of publications available including books, videos and CD-ROMs, which contain the entire pool of questions and answers. There's no real excuse for failing, but if you do you will have to resit the test.

When you pass, you will receive a certificate which you must produce to the examiner when you take your practical test. This certificate is valid for two years. If you have not taken and passed the practical test in that time you will have to resit the theory test.

## LICENCES AND ENTITLEMENTS

### Moped Riders

If you're settling for a moped, you can organise further road training and take the practical moped test. Once you pass the test, you will hold a full moped licence which will entitle you to ride without L-plates and carry a pillion passenger. If you take the test on an automatic, your licence will be restricted to automatic mopeds only.

### Motorcycle Riders

If you're aged between 17 and 20 years, you will limited to practising on a motorcycle up to 125cc engine capacity with a power output not exceeding 11 kW (14.6 bhp).

- If you pass the test on a machine between 75 cc and 125 cc you will be given a Light Motorcycle Licence (A1) and will be entitled to ride motorcycles up to 125 cc with a power output not exceeding 11 kW (14.6 bhp). You can ride without L-plates and carry a pillion passenger.

- If you pass the test on a machine between 121 cc and 125 cc that is capable of at least 100 kph (62 mph) you will be given a Standard Motorcycle Licence (A) and you will be restricted to riding a motorcycle with a power output not exceeding 25 kW (33.3 bhp). This restriction will apply for two years from the date of your test. After the two years have passed, you are automatically entitled to ride motorcycles of any size without taking a further test. It is hoped that the two-year restriction will allow you to gain experience of handling a medium-sized motorcycle in various road, weather and traffic conditions, and gain confidence at defensive riding, before you move on to a larger machine that is heavier and more powerful.

If you are aged 21 years or over, you are entitled to take the Direct Access Scheme route to a full unrestricted motorcycle licence (see Chapter 8 for details). You must take the test on a machine with a power output of at least 35 kW (46.6 bhp). A pass entitles you to ride any motorcycle without L-plates and carry a pillion passenger.

## TRAINING COURSES
### *Intensive Training Courses*

If you've got the cash and just want to get it all out of the way as soon as possible, go for intensive training. Many training companies provide these courses for both novices and previously experienced riders. A novice course will last about five to six days; most previously experienced riders will be ready for the test in three to four days. When booking such a course, it's important to make sure you are getting full days of suitable training and that the price includes such things as bike hire, comprehensive insurance and any test fees.

### *More Relaxed Courses*

If you want to take a more relaxed approach, go for the tailor-made courses provided by most training companies. It will take longer to get ready for your test but you will be able to spread the cost and practise between lessons. Don't leave long gaps between training sessions; if you get rusty you'll spend a lot of time relearning skills previously taught. If you need a learner motorcycle, some companies are able to loan you one, so you can practise between lessons. Always make sure the price includes bike hire, comprehensive insurance and any test fees.

You'll find that whichever route you decide to take, the cost will be similar.

## ELEMENTS THAT MUST BE PRACTISED

Whether you practise by yourself or go to a training company, you must gain experience riding on all types of road and in varied traffic conditions. Test routes are set so as to test your abilities when riding in urban areas with slower speed limits and more rural areas on faster roads and dual carriageways. Whichever path you take, you will need to practise the following:

- Moving off from the kerb
- Stopping at the kerb
- Changing gear
- Slow speed control
- U-turns
- Emergency stops
- Moving off on a hill
- Filtering
- Mirrors and rear observations

You must also know and practise the procedures for negotiating the following:

- Left and right turns
- Crossroads
- Box junctions
- Bends
- Roundabouts

- Traffic lights

- Pedestrian crossings

- Railway level crossings

- One-way streets

- Dual carriageways

- National speed limit roads

These items are described in detail below, with tips for safe riding.

## Moving Off from the Kerb

1. Sit at the side of the road with the engine running and in the safety position and with the rear brake applied.

2. Check in all directions for hazards. There's no point in thinking about moving off if an articulated lorry is bearing down on you.

3. When it looks as though it will be safe to move, lightly apply the front brake, put your right foot down for support, and select first gear.

4. Return to the safety position, putting your left foot down for support and applying the rear brake. Then release the front brake and leave your right hand free to control the throttle.

5. Increase the throttle and slowly release the clutch lever until you reach the biting point; the engine note will drop and to compensate you will need to increase the throttle slightly more.

6. Indicate if you think it will benefit other road users (including pedestrians).

7. When you're ready to move off, check in all directions for hazards, making sure you have a safe gap to move off into.

8. Look forward, release the rear brake and move smoothly away, gently releasing the clutch and steadily increasing the throttle.

9. Take up the correct road position, cancel the indicator and use the mirrors to check the situation behind.

10. Accelerate briskly up through the gears to a suitable speed within the set speed limit.

### Stopping at the Kerb

Before doing anything else, you need to find a safe place to stop. Places to avoid include no-waiting areas, the controlled areas of pedestrian crossings, outside schools, within 10 metres of a junction or opposite a junction, at a bus stop or blocking a driveway.

1. Once you've found your safe place, use your mirrors and consider a rear observation to check behind.

2. Signal left if it will benefit others; take care to avoid giving a misleading signal near junctions.

3. Take a left lifesaver look to make sure it's safe to move over.

4. Move to the left and then start to slow down.

5. Stop smoothly at the kerbside, using both brakes, and cancel the indicator.

6. Apply the front brake while you select neutral, and either return to the safety position or switch the engine off before dismounting and placing the machine on its stand.

## Changing Gear

Smooth gear-changing requires good co-ordination of the throttle, clutch and gear lever.

1. Position your foot under or over the gear lever.

2. Simultaneously close the throttle and pull in the clutch lever.

3. Change gear firmly.

4. Gently release the clutch and simultaneously increase the throttle to take up the drive in the new gear.

When changing down a gear, you may need to slow down to a suitable speed before engaging the lower gear. You can smooth out the change by blipping the throttle (giving it a quick twist to rev the engine slightly) just before releasing the clutch.

Practise finding first gear just as you stop. This is particularly important when stopping at junctions or traffic lights. If you haven't found first gear cleanly, you will be fumbling around with the gears, holding up following traffic and not making progress.

Practise changing smoothly up and down the gearbox, matching your speed and gear to the road and traffic conditions.

## Slow Speed Control

The ability to control a motorcycle at low speed is essential, particularly when travelling in heavily congested urban areas.

Find a safe off-road area to use for practice. If you are training with a riding school they will have an approved area suitable for practice. A good training course will include plenty of work in an off-road area to improve your clutch control and boost your confidence.

It might seem a bit silly riding around cones, but it all relates to safe road work and it pays off in the end. An imaginative instructor will make it good fun and your general machine-handling skills will improve greatly. If you're confident at controlling the motorcycle, you can spend more time concentrating on your road craft.

## U-Turns

Practise simulated U-turns on an off-road area before trying them on the public roads. Remember to make good observations in all directions before starting to turn, and don't set off until it's absolutely safe.

Don't pressure yourself. Settle down and be absolutely relaxed and comfortable before setting off.

1. Check both ways for hazards. There's little point in thinking about doing a U-turn if someone's just about to park opposite you.

2. Apply the front brake and select first gear before returning to the safety position with the rear brake applied. Let go of the front brake so your hand is free to control the throttle.

3. A signal is generally not required for a U-turn because there should be no one to signal to.

4. Increase the throttle and release the clutch lever to the biting point; the engine note will drop, so increase the throttle further to compensate.

5. Check in all directions and make sure it's absolutely safe before starting your turn.

6 Keeping the throttle busy and the clutch at the biting point, ride your machine in a right-hand curve, stopping next to the kerb on the opposite side of the road.

The following notes may help you:

• Gentle application of the rear brake will be sufficient to control your speed and maintain stability. Most roads have a camber for drainage; going up the camber you may not need the brake, but once you've passed the crown, you may need the brake coming down the camber on the other side of the road.

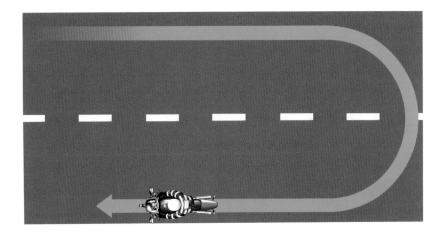

- If necessary, counterbalance the bike by shifting your body weight to the left.

- Don't look at the kerb or that's where you'll end up. Keep your head up and look down the road to where you want to stop.

- If the motorcycle starts to fall to the right, release the clutch a little to correct it.

- Don't use the front brake while turning, as it will cause the front wheel to dig in and you will overbalance and perhaps fall off.

## Emergency Stops

Bringing a motorcycle to a safe, controlled stop in an emergency is an essential skill. Practise simulated stops on a suitable off-road area before trying them on a public road. When practising on public roads, pick a quiet side road and make sure it's absolutely safe. A good training course will include plenty of practice both off and on the road.

1. Start by travelling at a realistic speed for the conditions.

2. Close the throttle and lose the engine power.

3. Apply the front brake first, quickly followed by the rear brake. Make the best use of the brakes to slow the machine as quickly as possible.

4. Just before you stop, pull the clutch in to prevent the engine stalling.

5. As you stop, put your left foot down; don't let go of the rear brake.

6. Quickly find first gear, check behind and ride over to the kerb.

Note the following:

- If you pull the clutch in too early, the rear wheel is disengaged from the drive. Because you are applying the rear brake, the rear wheel is likely to lock, causing a skid and loss of control.

- Avoid changing gear as you stop because pulling in the clutch increases the chances of locking the rear wheel.

## Moving Off on a Hill

You must be able to move off from a gradient safely and smoothly, without rolling backwards or stalling the engine.

When on a hill and using the centre stand, make sure you use the routine taught during CBT and the machine will always be under control. If you have a side stand, it may be more suitable to use this for parking on a hill. When stationary and sitting on the machine, always have a brake applied.

1. Apply the front brake while selecting first gear, then return to the safety position with the rear brake applied and your right hand free to control the throttle.

2. Increase the throttle and release the clutch to the biting point; the engine note will change and the back of the bike will settle down.

3. It will take more power to pull you up the hill, so increase the throttle considerably more than if you were setting off on the flat.

4. Check in all directions and make sure it's safe to set off, signalling if necessary.

5. Release the rear brake and providing the biting point has been found the motorcycle will move away. Gently release the clutch while increasing

the throttle. Feed the clutch out a lot more gently than you would on the flat and don't try to change up to second gear too early.

6. Accelerate away to your normal road position, cancel any signal and use the mirrors to check behind.

## Filtering

Filtering is a form of overtaking. It's generally not expected during the test (except in London). Being something of a contentious issue, it's not taught by many instructors; however, when done correctly it's safe and legal.

When traffic is stationary or slow-moving in queues, motorcyclists can filter slowly along the queue and make progress. The advantages of filtering must always be weighed against the increased risks.

- Make yourself visible, always take extreme care and travel slowly as you may need to stop quickly.

- Always be prepared to brake or use your horn and never stop in a driver's blind spot.

- Before moving out of the queue identify a space ahead where you can safely pull in.

- Never filter in the gutter between vehicles and the kerb.

- Always check behind before moving out, and watch out for other motorcyclists or pedal cyclists who may already be filtering.

- Understand that filtering to the front of a queue can upset drivers and may lead to a race-style start. Generally it's better to avoid any conflict by stopping a few vehicles back from the front of the queue.

- Watch for pedestrians crossing between vehicles and other vehicles emerging from junctions, and for vehicle doors opening or occupants leaning out.

- Expect vehicles to change lanes or U-turn without signalling.

- Road markings and 'cat's-eyes' (reflective studs) can throw the motorcycle off line.

- Remember all road signs and markings still apply.

## *Mirrors and Rear Observations*

You must always know what's happening behind you. Sensible use of the mirrors and rear observations will keep you informed. Use the mirrors regularly, remembering that they have blind spots and can distort the view.

It's difficult to accurately judge speed and distance using mirrors alone. When necessary, take effective rear observations over your shoulder. When making an observation give your eyes a chance to focus, in order to judge speed and distance accurately.

If necessary, take a lifesaver look over the appropriate shoulder before moving position or turning.

Remember that too many rear observations or badly timed observations can be dangerous.

## Left and Right Turns

Practise simulated left and right turns on an off-road area or on quiet side roads before venturing on to busier roads. Good training courses will include plenty of practice, both off and on the road.

The procedures for left and right turns are given in Chapter 5 (from page 78) as they form part of CBT. Make sure you:

- Know and understand the signs and road markings at junctions.

- Practise the OSM-PSL routines using a variety of junctions.

- Make good observations and signal and position correctly for each turn.

- Control the clutch and throttle as you turn, and maintain a safe course.

- Always cancel the indicators; failure to do this can be very dangerous.

## Crossroads

Make sure you recognise the signs, road markings and other clues that let you know there's a crossroads ahead.

1. Because you may have to slow down or move position on the approach to a crossroads junction, use your mirrors to check behind and if necessary take a rear observation.

2. Such things as parked vehicles, trees or hedges may block your view into the junction. If your view into the junction is poor, consider moving to the right to get a better view.

3. You may need to slow down, give way or stop. Consider using your horn to warn others of your presence.

4. Check both ways and, if it's safe, accelerate across.

Note the following:

- When negotiating a crossroads junction travelling along the major road, it may not be necessary to slow down; your speed will be governed by your view. Remember if the view is good and there's nothing coming, the traffic behind you will not be expecting you to slow down.

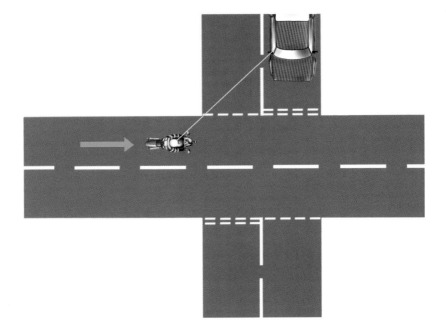

- An unmarked crossroads is where two roads of a similar size cross with no signs or road markings. These require extra caution because no one has priority, and they can be difficult to spot. The same system should be used on the approach, but if a vehicle is approaching from either direction you should give way. If another vehicle has given way to you, then proceed with caution and be prepared to stop if necessary.

- Use the correct system when turning right at crossroads (see pages 80 and 82). If an oncoming vehicle is also turning right, it's safer to turn behind each other because you both keep your view of the road ahead.

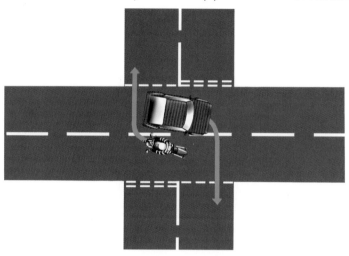

- If you are forced to turn in front of an oncoming vehicle, edge forwards until you get a good view before committing yourself to the turn.

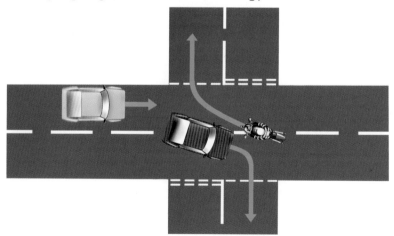

## Box Junctions

Box junctions are designed to avoid gridlock by keeping busy junctions clear. You may only enter a box junction if your exit is clear. If not you must remain outside the cross-hatched area. When turning right and your exit is clear, you may enter the box junction and wait for a gap in the oncoming traffic before completing your turn.

If there is already a queue of traffic in the box junction waiting to turn right, it would be sensible to wait outside the painted area until some of the queue in front of you clears.

## Negotiating Bends

You must practise the correct systems for safely negotiating bends. When travelling around a bend, you counteract the cornering forces and steer the motorcycle by leaning the machine to the left or the right as appropriate.

If you're travelling straight and apply gentle pressure to the right handlebar and push it away slightly, the motorcycle will lean to the right. If you gently push on the left handlebar, the machine will lean to the left. This is known as counter steering and riders often do it unconsciously without having to be taught. As you lean the motorcycle over, lean in the same direction and keep your body in line with the machine.

When a motorcycle is leaning ('banked over'), the tyre grip is reduced: if you bank it over too far the tyre grip may be lost altogether and the machine will skid.

Make sure you are familiar with all the signs, road markings and other clues on the approach to bends and assess each bend correctly.

1. If necessary slow down on the approach while travelling upright and straight. Having slowed down, select the correct gear for the bend.

2. Position correctly on the approach to the bend:

   - For a right-hand bend, it's best to position over to the left for the best view into the bend; don't ride in the gutter or on loose debris though, or you may skid. If you ride close to the centre line, your head and shoulders will hang into the opposite carriageway as you lean the machine over.

- For a left-hand bend, moving out towards the centre line can put you at risk from oncoming traffic, so keep to your normal riding position.

Your view into the bend won't be that good, so watch out for hazards such as a junction, parked vehicles or pedestrians.

3. As you negotiate the bend, cornering forces will reduce your speed, so accelerate gently to compensate and keep the motorcycle stable.

4. As the bend opens out, reduce your lean until you are upright, and accelerate away to a suitable speed.

Note the following:

- You should always be able to stop on your side of the road within the distance you can see to be clear.

- If you shut off the throttle in a bend, cornering forces will take over and the bike will be thrown outwards in the opposite direction to the turn.

## Camber and Super-elevation

The road camber can work for you by increasing tyre grip on a left-hand bend. On a right-hand bend, the camber can reduce tyre grip.

If the bend is super-elevated (banked), the banking works to increase tyre grip in both directions.

## Roundabouts

You will need to practise the routines for dealing with all kinds of roundabouts. Roundabouts are placed at busy junctions to ease the flow of traffic and you generally have to give way to traffic already on the roundabout. Be familiar with all the signs and road markings associated with roundabouts.

When negotiating a roundabout, you must be aware of the hazards on the road surface such as diesel fuel, manhole covers and the debris that collects in the disused areas. You should have learned about these as part of your Compulsory Basic Training.

### When Turning Left

There may be more than one exit going off to the left, but the only left turn is the first exit. If you approach with a left indicator on intending to leave by the second exit, you mislead other drivers entering the roundabout.

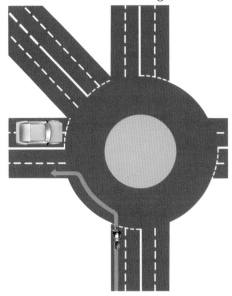

1. Use the mirrors and consider a rear observation to check the situation behind.

2. Signal left and approach in the left-hand lane. If there is only one lane, approach in your normal riding position.

3. Watch the traffic on the roundabout and try to adjust your speed to arrive when there's a suitable gap.

4. Enter the roundabout and keep to the left. Leave by the first exit and cancel your indicator.

### When Going Straight On

Exits between the left turn and straight on should be treated the same as straight on.

1. Use your mirrors and consider a rear observation to check the situation behind.

2. Don't signal on the approach.

3. Unless road markings direct you otherwise, approach in the left-hand lane. If there is only one lane, maintain your normal riding position. On some roundabouts there may be two lanes for going straight on. If the left lane is blocked, use the next available one to the right.

4. Watch the traffic on the roundabout and try to adjust your speed to arrive when there's a suitable gap.

5. Keep to the left unless road markings indicate otherwise. Don't ride on the debris in the disused areas.

6. Signal left as you pass the exit before the one you're taking and take a lifesaver look to make sure it's safe to exit the roundabout.

7. Cancel your indicator once you've left the roundabout.

## When Turning Right

All exits beyond straight on should be treated as a right turn unless road markings dictate otherwise.

1. Use your mirrors and consider a rear observation to check the situation behind.

2. Signal right on the approach and maintain this signal on the roundabout.

3. Approach in the right-hand lane. If there is only one lane, position to the right.

4. Watch the traffic on the roundabout and try to adjust your speed to arrive when there's a suitable gap.

5. Enter the roundabout and keep to the right, but not too close to the island as this part of the road is often dirty.

6. Signal left as you pass the exit before the one you're taking and take a lifesaver look to make sure it's safe to leave the roundabout.

7. Cancel your indicator once you've left the roundabout.

## Aborting a Manoeuvre

If you decide it's unsafe to leave by your chosen exit, it can be dangerous to slow down or stop on a roundabout. It may be safer to abort the manoeuvre. Check to the right and signal right, continue around the roundabout and try again.

## Lifesaver Observations on Roundabouts

If you feel at risk when negotiating a roundabout, take a lifesaver look in the appropriate direction. Remember it can be dangerous to look away at the wrong moment.

## Large Roundabouts

Large roundabouts at busy interchanges require extra vigilance because of the extra lanes and the volume of traffic.

Observe the route signs and road markings and position in the correct lane in good time on the approach. Watch for vehicles cutting across your path, and for any changes in priority as sometimes there are give way markings on the roundabout.

The traffic on some roundabouts will be controlled by traffic lights, which may operate only at peak times.

## Mini-roundabouts

These are placed at smaller busy junctions and there's less space in which to do all the observations and signals. Be familiar with the road signs and markings for mini-roundabouts.

Other vehicles such as buses and lorries may drive over the painted spot. However, you must avoid riding over the painted area as it's very slippery, particularly when wet.

Watch for drivers who signal incorrectly or use the island for a U-turn.

### Traffic Lights

You must be able to recognise all types of traffic light signals. Study the Highway Code and understand the sequence and meaning of traffic lights.

- A red light means stop and wait behind the white stop line until the green light shows.

- Red and amber lights together also mean stop and wait. You must not pass the stop line until the green shows.

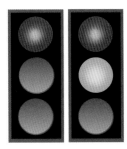

- A green light means you may go, but only if the way is clear. Remember, you should approach green traffic lights at a speed that will allow you to stop safely if the lights change.

- A green arrow filter light may be provided to allow the movement of traffic in a certain direction. The green filter phase can be at the beginning or end of the green phase.

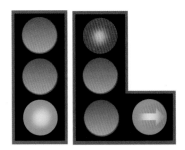

- Amber means stop at the stop line. You may continue only if amber appears after you have passed the stop line, or if you are so close that if you were to stop it would be dangerous.

- White horizontal and vertical traffic lights may be provided for trams.
- When travelling straight on or using a dedicated lane at traffic lights, it is best to dominate your lane by riding in the centre of the lane. This prevents any other vehicles from driving or stopping alongside you in your lane.

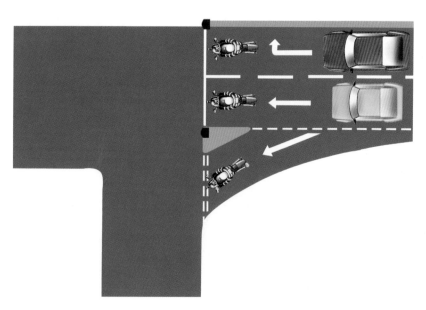

## Pedestrian Crossings

You must be familiar with the meaning of the lights and the road markings at all types of pedestrian crossing.

- You must not park on a crossing or on the painted zig-zag areas.

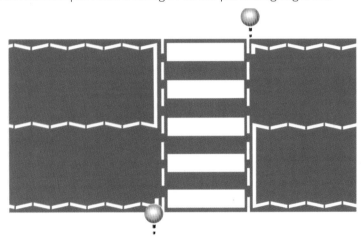

- You must not overtake the leading vehicle on the approach to a crossing, whether that vehicle is moving or has stopped to give way to pedestrians.

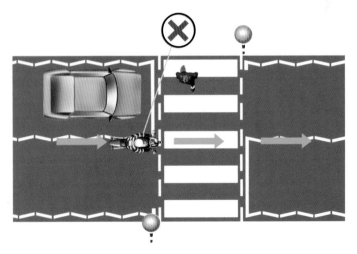

- When in a traffic queue you must not stop on the crossing.

- You must always stop and give way to pedestrians who are already crossing or who are about to cross.

- You must approach a crossing at a speed that will allow you to stop safely if necessary.

- While negotiating a pedestrian crossing, take up a dominant lane position to give you a better view and prevent other drivers from overtaking or stopping alongside you.

### Zebra Crossings

You can recognise a zebra crossing in the distance by the flashing orange beacons. If there are people crossing or waiting to cross you should stop and give way. Watch out for pedestrians trying to cross within the zig-zag area.

The painted areas can be very slippery, particularly when wet.

### Pelican Crossings

These are light-controlled crossings and you must stop when the red light shows. When the flashing amber light shows, you must give way to any pedestrians who are already crossing. If there are no pedestrians crossing you may go, but with caution.

Don't try to intimidate pedestrians by edging forward or revving your engine.

### Puffin Crossings

This newer type of light-controlled crossing looks similar to a Pelican crossing but does not have a flashing amber phase. This is because it is equipped with sensors to detect the pedestrians and should not change while pedestrians are crossing.

Red and amber means stop. You must not cross the stop line until the crossing is clear and the green light shows.

The red and green man signs are mounted above the push button, so the pedestrians can see them clearly.

### Toucan Crossings

These light-controlled crossings combine a pedestrian crossing with a cycle lane crossing, hence the name 'Two can'. There is no flashing amber phase.

### Pegasus Crossings

These light-controlled crossings are provided for horse riders where a bridle path crosses a road. Expect to find these near racecourses or stables. The push button is much higher so the rider can reach it without dismounting.

## *Railway Level Crossings*

You must be familiar with all the signals, road signs and markings associated with railway level crossings.

- You must not cross if the red lights show, or if the alarm is sounding or the barriers are dropping. Do not swerve around half barriers as a train is likely to pass.

- If the red lights show you must stop behind the white stop line. If you have passed the line when the amber light shows, keep going.

- Do not park or overtake on the approach to a level crossing.

- At crossings with no lights or barriers, look both ways and continue only if it's absolutely safe. If a telephone is provided, use it to contact the signalman.

## One-way Streets

You must be familiar with all the signs and clues that indicate a one-way street. If you don't know you are in a one-way street it can be very dangerous, particularly when turning right.

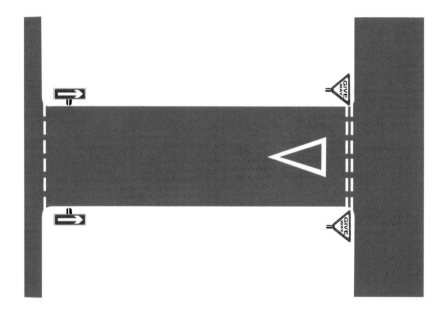

As you turn into a one-way street you will find that any parked vehicles will be facing in the same direction. Make sure you take note of any signs and road markings and position in the correct lane as soon as possible.

You must only travel in the direction indicated, although there may be a contraflow, bus or cycle lane.

When travelling in a dedicated lane it's best to ride in the centre of the lane to prevent other drivers driving alongside you in the same lane.

When turning right at the end of a one-way street, being further away from the right-hand kerb will give you a better view into the junction.

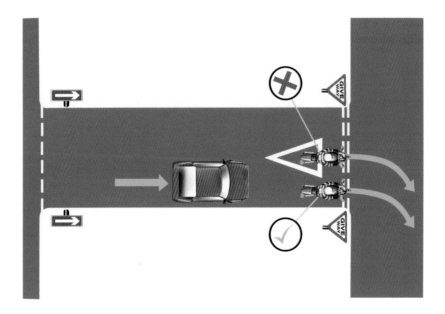

## Dual Carriageways

You must be familiar with all the road signs and markings associated with dual carriageways.

Dual carriageways have a central reserve (or reservation) dividing the carriageways. The speed limit is often set higher on dual carriageways than on other roads, but this is not always the case.

## Turning Left on to a Dual Carriageway

- If there is no acceleration lane, you should turn as you would normally, using the OSM-PSL routine. Be careful as traffic may be travelling faster than usual.

- If there is an acceleration lane, you should use it to build up your speed to match that of the traffic flow. Signal right, take a right lifesaver look, and move into a safe gap in the traffic.

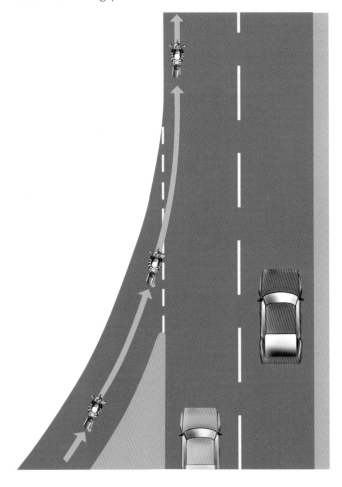

### Turning Left from a Dual Carriageway

1. Make sure you spot any signs or countdown markers in plenty of time.

2. If there is no deceleration lane, you should turn as usual using the OSM-PSL routine and making sure you signal and slow down in plenty of time.

   If there is a deceleration lane, you should signal in plenty of time and use the deceleration lane to slow down. Slowing down on the main carriageway will hold up the traffic flow.

3. If you've been riding at high speed, check your speedometer. You may be going faster than you think.

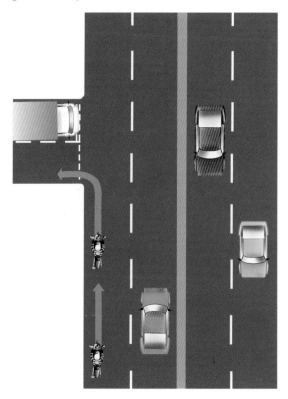

### Turning Right on to a Dual Carriageway

1. Use the usual OSM-PSL routine on the approach.

2. If the central reserve is wide enough to wait in, you can treat the carriageways as two separate roads:

   • Look for a safe gap on the first carriageway and emerge to wait in the protected area of the central reserve.

   • Now wait for a suitable gap on the second carriageway before emerging to turn safely on to the left-hand lane. Remember a right lifesaver look will spot anyone trying to cut across on your right.

   If the central reserve is too narrow, you must wait patiently for a safe gap in both directions before emerging.

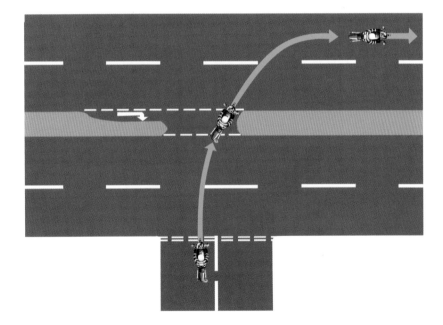

### Turning Right from a Dual Carriageway

1. Make sure you spot any signs or countdown markers in plenty of time.

2. Position in the outside lane and signal in plenty of time on the approach.

3. If there is a filter lane, get into it as soon as possible and try to slow down out of the traffic flow.

4. The traffic on the opposite carriageway may be travelling quickly, so make sure you have a large gap. If in doubt wait.

5. Remember the value of a lifesaver look before turning.

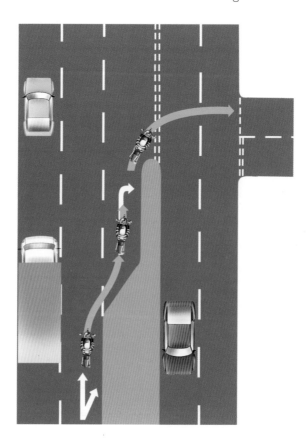

## Lane Discipline

- Always change lane safely without forcing other road drivers or riders to swerve or slow down. Before changing lanes, use your mirrors and take a lifesaver look to check the blind spot before signalling and moving across when safe.

- Make sure you spot any signs and road markings in plenty of time and get into lane early. Do not change lanes unnecessarily.

- On a two-lane dual carriageway you should travel in the left-hand lane; the right-hand lane is for overtaking. If you use the right-hand lane you should move back into the left-hand lane as soon as possible.

- On a three-lane dual carriageway and on motorways, you should travel in the left-hand lane; the middle and right-hand lanes are for overtaking. If you use the middle or right-hand lanes, return to the middle lane and then the left-hand lane as soon as possible.

- You must not park or ride in bus or cycle lanes marked with a solid white line during their hours of operation.

## Overtaking on Dual Carriageways

1. Plan well ahead and make sure it's safe to overtake. Don't attempt it if you're in any doubt.

2. Make sure your machine has enough reserve speed to overtake briskly.

3. Look beyond the vehicle you want to overtake and make sure there's a safe gap to move into once you've completed the manoeuvre.

4. Use your mirrors and consider a rear observation to check the situation behind.

5. Position so you can see well beyond the vehicle you're about to overtake.

6. Look ahead and make sure the lane you're moving into is clear.

7. If it's safe to overtake, check behind again, signal, and move out.

8. Overtake briskly, cancel your signal, and return to the left lane without cutting in on the vehicle you've overtaken.

### National Speed Limit Roads

You must be familiar with the national speed limits for motorcycles on single carriageway roads, dual carriageways and motorways. The national speed limit on single carriageways is 60 mph. On national speed limit dual carriageways and motorways it's 70 mph.

If it's safe, you must make reasonable progress on fast roads. It can be dangerous to travel at 30 mph when following traffic is travelling at 70 mph.

## Pillion Passengers

Learner riders must not carry a pillion passenger. However, it is useful to know what to do and how carrying a passenger can affect a machine, especially as you will be asked about this during your motorcycle test.

Carrying a pillion passenger can affect the way your motorcycle handles. You need to be aware of the effects and how to deal with them, including making any necessary adjustments to your machine, before you take a passenger on board.

If you are carrying a pillion passenger you might want to make the following adjustments to the machine:

- Adjust the rear suspension settings.

- Increase the rear tyre pressure.

- Adjust the mirrors and headlight.

Carrying a pillion passenger will affect the handling characteristics of the motorcycle. The added weight will impair acceleration and it will take longer to stop.

### Advice for a Pillion Passenger
Ensure your passenger knows what to do, especially if they have no previous experience of motorcycle riding.

- Wear an approved safety helmet properly fastened, and dress sensibly.

- Sit astride the machine facing forwards with your feet on the footrests, and keep them there even when stationary.

- Hold on to the grab rail or the rider.

- In bends, lean with the machine, not against it.

- Don't move about or give arm signals.

The Direct Access Scheme (DAS) was introduced in 1997 and is open to learners who are aged 21 or over. It is designed so that you can train and take your test on a larger machine, and therefore move straight to an unrestricted licence. Direct Access training costs more than training to pass on a 125 cc motorcycle because of the increased insurance premiums.

Before committing yourself to training under this scheme you need to think about the sort of motorcycle you want to ride after passing your test. If you only want to ride a small commuter machine it is pointless to pay extra for Direct Access. Some people are quite happy to pass their test on a 125 cc motorcycle and spend two years restricted to machines with a power output not exceeding 25 kW (33 bhp).

It is possible to fit a restrictor kit to any large motorcycle and restrict its power output to these limits. However, the cost of buying and fitting these kits is similar to the extra cost of training on the Direct Access Scheme.

It is possible to use your own motorcycle for Direct Access; however, the cost of insurance during training can be prohibitive, so most people hire a machine from their training company.

Most training companies structure their courses so you complete CBT and perhaps some further road training on a 125 cc motorcycle before you graduate to the larger DAS motorcycles (power output at least 35 kW or 46.6 bhp).

When practising under the Direct Access Scheme you must always be accompanied by a qualified DAS instructor on another motorcycle.

You must be in radio contact and wear fluorescent or reflective clothing. You must display L-plates correctly and comply with all other provisional licence restrictions.

## ACCELERATED ACCESS

If you are aged over 21 years and you have a restricted licence, you can train on a larger machine and take your test for an unrestricted licence. If you have a restricted licence and turn 21 years during your two-year restricted period, you can train and take your test on a larger machine to gain an unrestricted licence. The same conditions apply as for Direct Access training.

## DIRECT ACCESS OR ACCELERATED ACCESS TRAINING

If you have previously trained on a smaller motorcycle, your instructor will familiarise you with the new larger motorcycle and explain the use of any additional controls or features.

The larger motorcycle is much more powerful:

- The throttle will be more responsive. The motorcycle will accelerate much more quickly and is capable of very high speeds.

- It will have much more powerful brakes to slow it down very quickly. Larger machines may have linked braking systems or ABS (anti-lock braking systems).

- Indelicate use of the controls can be very dangerous.

The larger motorcycle is heavier, longer and maybe wider:

- The weight can aid stability once the machine is moving but it can be a problem when walking with the machine or putting it on the stand.

- It may have a reduced turning circle and will require more space when manoeuvring or parking.

You should practise on a safe off-road area so you can get used to the handling characteristics of the larger motorcycle before venturing on to public roads.

Once on the public roads you will need to practise all the elements mentioned in Chapter 6 until you're confidently handling the larger machine in all traffic conditions. Discuss your riding with your instructor and listen to his or her opinion as to whether you are ready to take the practical test.

## HOW TO BOOK YOUR TEST

Most training companies will have prebooked a test for you and the cost (approximately £45) will have been included in the course price.

If necessary you can apply for a motorcycle test by:

- Post: Complete an application form (DL26), which you can get from any driving test centre or your training company. Send it with the fee to the address given on the form.

- Telephone: Call the DSA booking centre (0870 0101 372). They accept most major credit cards. You may have to wait some time during busy periods as this line is used for all driving test bookings and enquiries, for both motorcycles and cars.

Make sure you apply in plenty of time to avoid disappointment and inform the booking department of any special circumstances that may affect the test, such as deafness or any disability. Arrangements can be made for non-English speakers.

Within two weeks you should receive your test appointment card with the time and location of your test. If the appointment isn't suitable and you want to postpone or cancel the test, you must do so within ten working days.

Some driving test centres can provide tests on Saturdays or weekday evenings, although these tests will cost more. Contact the DSA booking centre for details.

## THE DOCUMENTS YOU NEED

When you arrive at the test centre make sure you have the following:

- Driving Licence: make sure your personal details are correct, it has the proper motorcycle entitlement and it's signed. If you have a photo licence you must bring the paper counterpart, which is part of the licence.

- Theory Test Pass Certificate: if applicable.

- CBT Certificate: you must show this to the examiner. If you don't have it you will be unable to take the test, and will lose the test fee.

- Photographic Identity: you will need an acceptable form of photo identification such as a passport, an ID card issued by your employer or a bus pass. (Holders of the new photo licence do not need additional photographic ID.)

## YOUR TEST MOTORCYCLE

Make sure that the motorcycle you're using for the test is:

- Displaying L-plates of the correct size, which are clearly visible front and back. (D-plates may be used in Wales.)

- Roadworthy and legal and if necessary has a current MOT certificate.

- Correctly insured for your use.

- Of the engine size or power output for the test that you're taking.

- Displaying a current Vehicle Excise Licence disc.

## THE EXAMINERS

All examiners are human and they have good and bad days like all of us. They are all trained by the DSA and supervised regularly to maintain the same standard of testing. They do not have quotas for passing or failing test candidates. The examiner wants you to pass: whether you do is entirely up to you on the day.

## THE TEST ROUTES

Your test will be conducted over one of a number of approved test routes. The route will cover a wide variety of roads and traffic conditions and where possible will include dual carriageways and higher speed limits.

## THE FORMAT OF THE TEST

The practical motorcycle test lasts about 40 minutes, and in that time the examiner will expect to see you ride competently and safely in a variety of traffic conditions. The format of the test is the same for all classes of motorcycle.

### Documents and Radios

Make sure you arrive in good time for your appointment and wait in the waiting room for the examiner to call your name. Make sure you use the toilet if you need it! You'll be asked to produce your documentation and sign a declaration saying your motorcycle is insured. The examiner will kit you out with the one-way radio set used to direct you during the test; they'll be similar to the ones your instructor used.

## Eyesight Check

You'll have your eyesight checked. You must be able to read a number plate in good daylight at a minimum distance of 20.5 metres (about 67 feet). It's the same check you will have done during CBT, and if you normally wear glasses or contact lenses you must wear them.

## The Ride

The examiner usually rides another motorcycle but sometimes a car may be used. You will be asked to set off and the examiner will direct you over the radio. You should follow the road ahead unless the examiner or road signs tell you otherwise.

You will be expected to ride for yourself. At junctions and roundabouts you only have to find a gap big enough for you to emerge; don't worry about the examiner, just make good progress. If you get away from the examiner, you will be asked to find a safe place to wait before continuing the ride.

If you have problems with the radio, tap your helmet with your left hand and find somewhere safe to stop so the examiner can sort it out.

## Wrong Turns

If in your nervousness you take a wrong turn, you should complete the turn safely and wait somewhere safe for further directions from the examiner. Suddenly changing direction in the middle of a turn is dangerous and will cause you to fail the test.

## Special Exercises

At some point (usually early on) the examiner will ask you to complete the following exercises:

- Emergency Stop: The examiner will ask you to ride a short circuit and at some point on that circuit you will be signalled to stop. The signal will only be given if it's safe.

- Walking with the Machine: You will be asked to place the motorcycle on its stand and then take it off again. You'll then be asked to walk with the machine without the aid of the engine.

- U-turn: You will be asked to complete a safe U-turn in the road and stop at the opposite kerb.

- Angle Start: The examiner will ask you to stop just before a parked vehicle and then move off safely. If an angle start occurs normally during the test you may not be asked to do the set exercise.

- Hill Start: The examiner will ask you to stop on a hill and then set off safely on the incline. If a hill start occurs normally on the test you may not be asked to complete the set exercise.

- Slow Riding: The examiner will ask you to ride a short distance at walking pace. If you have already ridden slowly during the test you may not be asked to complete the set exercise.

During the test you will be expected to ride competently and safely, using speed sensibly and making good progress. Making minor errors will not necessarily cause you to fail the test, although if you make enough of them you will. Aim for perfection but don't go to pieces if you make a mistake; you may still be able to redeem yourself.

At the end of the ride, the examiner will ask you questions relating to carrying pillion passengers on a motorcycle. Make sure you know the effect of carrying passengers, what you should advise them, and what adjustments may be required to the motorcycle (see page 141).

## IF YOU PASS

Congratulations! Once you've finished celebrating, make sure you complete an application for a new licence and send it together with your pass certificate and driving licence to the DVLA at Swansea. It's not unknown for post to be mislaid, so photocopy them before you send them off (you must send the originals). When you get your new licence, don't sign it until you have checked it has the correct entitlement.

## IF YOU FAIL

It's not the end of the world! Listen to any explanation given by the examiner and make sure you work hard on any faults. Discuss it with your instructor and arrange some further training before rebooking a further test. Don't leave it too long or you'll get rusty and have to relearn a lot of skills.

## FURTHER TRAINING

Just because you've passed your test it doesn't mean you know everything about safe riding. Remember, you only have to ride to a basic safe standard to pass the DSA test.

Now you need to improve those basic skills by taking further training. There are many courses available through training companies and other organisations such as the Institute of Advanced Motorists (IAM) or the Royal Society for the Prevention of Accidents (RoSPA). Any advanced training will usually lead to discounts on your insurance premiums and will certainly improve your skills and make riding more enjoyable.

Remember, if you want to keep riding and stay out of the accident statistics you must always learn from your mistakes. I hope this book has helped you on your way to a full bike licence. Enjoy yourself and maybe I'll see you at a bike meet one day. Happy riding!

# MOTORCYCLING TERMS AND ABBREVIATIONS

You may come across the following words, abbreviations or expressions in this book, in motorcycle publications and advertisements, or in conversation with other motorcyclists. If you encounter other terms you do not understand when training, ask your instructor to explain them.

| | |
|---|---|
| AAS | Accelerated Access Scheme. Allows those over 21 who hold a restricted licence to train for a full unrestricted licence without a two-year wait. |
| ATB | Approved Training Body. A company approved and licensed by the DSA as a motorcycle training organisation. |
| automatic | A motorcycle or moped that does not require the rider to change gear. |
| banked over | When the motorcyde is leaned right over, such as on a sharp bend. Also called 'cranked over' or 'knee-down'. |
| bars, bar ends | Handlebars. |
| bhp | Brake horse power; the effective power of the motor in an engine. |
| biting point | The point at which the clutch plates engage and the motorcycle is ready to move, and at which you can apply the throttle to accelerate. |
| blind spot | An area behind or to the side of you that you cannot see in your mirrors. |
| blip the throttle | A quick twist of the throttle to provide additional power. |
| body armour | Items of, or inserts for, clothing designed to protect you in an accident. |
| busy | An engine becomes more 'busy' as the throttle is increased. |
| camber | The convex structure of many roads which are lower at the sides than in the centre, primarily to assist drainage. |
| CBT | Compulsory Basic Training. You must pass CBT before you can apply for or train for your motorcycle test. |
| cc | Cubic centimetres; a measurement of engine capacity. |
| chinbar | The part of a full-face motorcycle helmet that protects the cheeks, lower face and chin. |
| cranked over | See 'banked over'. |
| DAS | Direct Access Scheme. Allows those over 21 to train and pass the test on a larger motorcycle to obtain a full unrestricted licence and avoid a two-year wait. |
| datatag® | A security system which electronically codes specific parts of your motorcycle in case of theft. |

| | |
|---|---|
| dirt bike | Another term for trail/trials bike. |
| driving point | See 'biting point'. |
| dropped | Crashed or fallen over. |
| DETR | Department of the Environment, Transport and the Regions. Government department responsible for road development and vehicle regulation. |
| DSA | Driving Standards Agency. Government body responsible for the training and testing of motorcyclists, drivers and driving instructors in the UK. |
| DVLA | Driver and Vehicle Licensing Agency. Government body responsible for the licensing and registration of vehicles, including motorcycles. |
| excess | The amount of any insurance claim that you have to pay yourself. |
| fairing | Streamlined external fittings (usually plastic) on a motorcycle to improve aerodynamics and reduce drag. |
| filtering | In heavy, slow-moving traffic, moving between other vehicles to the front of the queue. |
| footpeg | Another term for footrest. |
| grab rail | A rail, bar or handle at the rear of the pillion seat for a passenger to hold. |
| green-laning | Riding on unmade roads, tracks or country lanes. |
| hard-tail | A term used to describe cruiser-style bikes with no rear suspension. |
| headstock | The point at which the frame joins the front section of the motorcycle. |
| Kevlar® | Lightweight, but extremely strong, synthetic fibre used in motorcycle clothing, helmets and parts. |
| kill switch | The stop/go switch used to kill the power to the engine. |
| knee-down | See 'banked over'. |
| Kph | Kilometres per hour. |
| kW | Kilowatts; a measurement of electrical power now used to express engine power rather than bhp. |
| lid | Helmet. |
| lifesaver look | A final glance into a blind spot before changing position or turning. |
| logbook | The registration document (V5) which contains details of the machine and its owner. |
| main stand | Another term for centre stand. |
| moped | Small motorcycle with an engine smaller than 50cc and a maximum speed of 31 mph. |

| | |
|---|---|
| OSMPSL | Observation, Signal, Manouevre, Position, Speed, Look. |
| pillion | The rear part of the motorcycle seat, behind the rider, which may be used to carry a passenger or luggage. Also used to mean a passenger carried on this seat. |
| public roads | Any road adopted and maintained by the local council or the Highways Agency on which traffic may pass freely. |
| restrictor kit | Parts used to restrict the engine power of a motorcycle, usually to comply with legislation or licence terms. |
| road-legal | A bike or part that is acceptable by law for use on public roads. |
| salopettes | Leather motorcycle trousers with a high waist and shoulder straps. |
| scooter | Not the same as a moped, having a larger engine and no specific speed limitation. |
| sliders | Heavy-duty pads which attach to the outside of motorcycle leathers to avoid damaging the knees when taking sharp corners. Required only for racing. |
| soft-tail | A term used to describe cruiser-style bikes with rear suspension. |
| SORN | Statutory Off-Road Notification. A document used to declare that a vehicle is kept and used off-road only. |
| super-elevation | Banking of the road at a bend on which one side of the road is higher than the other. |
| tick-over | When the engine is running gently without the throttle being applied. |
| Vehicle Excise Licence | The official name for the tax disc. |
| wet gear | Another name for waterproofs. |

Accelerated access 144–5
accelerator (throttle) 52
alcohol 10, 100
alertness 13
  see also concentration
angle start 151
anticipation 13, 98
  see also concentration
Approved Training Bodies (ATBs) 17
attitude 9, 16, 98
  defensive 15
automatics (rev and go) 22
  moving off 68
  starting 66

banking 122
batteries, checking 65
bends 119–22
bikes see motorcycles
blind spots 70
body armour 46
boots see footwear
box junctions 119
brakes
  applying 68–9
  checking 64
  front lever 52
  rear lever 53
braking 68–9
  when stationary 69
British Standards
  helmets 42
  visors and goggles 45

cables, checking 64
camber 122
CBT certificate (DL 196) 32, 102, 148
centre stand 57–60
Certificate of Completion (DL 196) 32, 102,
  148
checks
  daily 63
  weekly 63–5
choke lever 55
cleaning 65
clothing 39–40
  protective 46-8
  visibility of 88–98
  see also individual types e.g. gloves
clutch
  control at junctions 84
  lever 57

commuters (bikes) 23
Compulsory Basic Training (CBT) 17, 39–40,
  41–102
  certificate 32, 102, 148
  course structure 40
  preparing for 39–40
concentration 9–10
controls 16, 49–57
cooling system, checking 65
counter-steering 119
crossings
  pedestrian 129–31
  railway 132
crossroads 116–18
custom cruisers 26

D-plates 33
Direct Access Scheme (DAS) 17, 105, 143–5
distance 93
DL 196 (CBT Certificate) 32, 102, 148
drive chain, checking 65
driving licence 29, 104–5
  mopeds 20, 34, 104
  motorcycles 35–6, 104–5
  steps towards getting 32, 34, 37
Driving Standards Agency (DSA) 17, 147
drugs, 10, 100
dual carriageways 134–40
  lane discipline 139
  overtaking on 139–40
  turning left from 136
  turning left on to 135
  turning right from 138
  turning right on to 137

electric starter button 53
emergency stops 75–8, 112–13, 151
  common faults 77–8
engine 66
engine stop switch 52
equipment, visibility of 89
European Standards
  body armour 47
  helmets 42–5
  visors or goggles 45–6
examiners 149
eyes
  protection 45–6
  sight test 41, 150
eyesight check 41, 150

fatigue 10, 100

field of view 10–11
filtering 114–15
　see also overtaking
fog 94
footwear 48
fuel and oil on the road 94
fuel tap 54

gauntlets see gloves and gauntlets
gear changing 72–3, 109
　common faults 73
gear lever 56
glasses 40
gloves and gauntlets 48
goggles see visors and goggles
gravel and debris 96

hazards
　action to avoid 12
　categories of 12
　spotting 12–13, 98
headlights 89
helmets
　British Standard 42
　buying 43
　construction 43
　European Standard 42
　fasteners 44
　full-face 42
　lifespan and care 45
　one-impact 43
　open-face 43
　visibility of 89
Highway Code 100
hill starts 113–14, 151
horn 50
hydraulic hoses, checking 64

ignition switch 51
illness 10, 100
indicator switch 50
Institute of Advanced Motorists (IAM) 152
instrument panel 51
insurance 29–30

jackets 46, 47
junctions 78–86, 116–26
　assessing 80
　box 119
　clutch control at 84
　common faults at 86
　completing turns at 85

obstructed view at 84
signalling at 85

kerb
　moving off from 107–8
　stopping at 108
kick-start lever 54
kite-mark see British Standards
Know Your Traffic Signs 100

L-plates 33
lane discipline 139
law 29–37, 87
　possible changes to 37
learner-legal motorcycles 21
learners 21
　licence 32
leaves 97
leathers see clothing
licences, types of 29, 104–5
　learner's 32
　Light Motorcycle Licence (A1) 104
　moped 34, 104
　motorcycles 35–6, 104–5
　provisional 102
　restricted 144
　steps towards getting 33–6
　unrestricted Motorcycle Licence 105,
　　143–4
lifesaver observations 12, 70, 92
light switches 50
logbook (Registration Document) 30
lubrication 65

machine control 16
manhole covers 96
manoeuvres 78–86
　turning left and right 78–86
　see also junctions, roundabouts, turns
mini-roundabouts 126
mirrors 92, 115
Module A (CBT) 41–8
Module B (CBT) 49–66
Module C (CBT) 67–86
Module D (CBT) 87–100
Module E (CBT) 101-102
mopeds 20
　licence for 104
　steps to getting a full licence 34
MOT (Vehicle Test Certificate) 30
motorcycle test 147, 152

motorcycles
  buying 28
  choosing 19
  costs 19, 28
  larger bikes 144–5
  safety checks 63–5
  steps to getting a full licence 35–6
  test bikes 39, 148
  types 20–7
  walking with 65–6, 151
  wheeling 65–6, 151
motorcyclists 9
  vulnerability 88–9
moving off 67–71
  angle start 151
  common faults 71
  from the kerb 107–8
  on a hill 113–14, 151
moving slowly 73–5, 110, 151

national speed limit roads 140

observations 10–12, 98
  focused 11
  lifesaver 12, 70–1, 92
  rear 11, 70–1, 92, 115
  scanning 12
off-roaders (trail bikes) 27
oil
  checking 64
  on road 90, 95
one-way streets 133–4
OSM-PSL routine 78–82
overtaking
  dual carriageways 139–40
  positioning 92
  see also filtering

parking
  downhill facing 62
  see also stands
passengers (pillion) 141, 152
patience 14
pedestrian crossings 129–31
pegasus crossings 131
pelican crossings 130
pillion passengers 141–2, 152
planning 14
positioning 90–1
  bends 120
  dual carriageways 138–9
puffin crossings 131

radios
  use in test 149, 150
  use in training 101
railway level crossings 132
rear observations 11, 70–1, 92, 115
Registration Document (V5) 30
responsibility 16
riding
  defensively 99
  on-road 87–100, 101–2
  on-site 67–86
road rage 9, 14–5, 99
road markings 97
road repairs 97
road surfaces 76, 90, 95-7
  uneven 96
road tax (Vehicle Excise Duty) 31
roundabouts 123–6
  going straight on at 124
  large 126
  mini 126
  positioning at 90, 123–5
  signalling at 123–5
  turning left at 123–4
  turning right at 125
Royal Society for the Prevention of Accidents
  (RoSPA) 152–3

safety helmets see helmets
safety position 69
scanning 12
scooters 23
side stand 57, 61–2, 113
signals
  brake lights 89
  cancelling 85
  misleading 85
  at roundabouts 123–5
skid control 76–7
slow control 73–5, 110, 151
snow and ice 95
special exercises 151
speed 97–8
  national speed limit roads 140
  slow speed control 73–5, 110, 151
sports bikes 24
standards see British Standards; European
  Standards
stands 57–8, 113
  centre stand 57–60
  side stand 61–2
starter button 53

starting
    angle start 151
    electric starter button 53
    engine 66
    hill starts 113–14, 151
    kick-start lever 54
    see also moving off
steering
    counter-steering 119
    lock 51
stopping 66, 68–71
    at the kerb 108
    common faults 71
    emergency 75–7, 112–13
sunlight 94
super-elevation 122
suspension, checking 64

tests (motorcycle) 147–52
    booking 147
    documents needed for 148
    failing 152
    passing 152
    see also Compulsory Basic Training (CBT)
tests (theory) 103
tests (Vehicle Test, MOT) 30
theory test 103
throttle (accelerator) 52
toucan crossings 131
tourers (bikes) 25
traffic
    filtering through 114–15
    riding in 22, 73–4
traffic lights 127–8
trail bikes (off-roaders) 27
training 17–18
    Accelerated Access 144–5
    bodies 17–18
    courses 143
    Direct Access Scheme (DAS) 17, 105,
        143–5
    further 152–3

intensive courses 105–7
    on-road 101–102
    ordinary courses 105–7
    see also Compulsory Basic Training
trousers 47
turning 78–86, 116–26
    common faults 86
    completing 85
    left into a major road 80
    left into a minor road 82
    right into a major road 80–81
    right into a minor road 83–4
    U-turns 110–12, 151
    see also dual carriageways; junctions;
        roundabouts
two-second rule 93
tyres, checking 64

U-turns 110–2, 151
uneven road surfaces 96

Vehicle Excise Duty (road tax) 31
Vehicle Test Certificate (MOT) 30
view, obstruction of 11, 84
visibility (of riders) 89
visors and goggles
    British Standard 45–6
    cleaning 46
    European Standard 46
    tinted 46

waterproofs 47, 48
weather 10, 94–5
wet conditions 94
wet leaves 97
wheeling motorcycles 65–6
wheels
    checking 64
    see also skid control
wind 94

zebra crossings 130

## MOTORCYCLE CITY BRANCHES AT:

Bristol Brislington

Bristol Central

Manchester

Newton Abbot

Paddock Wood

Portsmouth

Reading

Shipley

Southampton

Tamworth

Wells


London Branches:

Battersea SW11

Bedfont TW14

Clapham SW4

Great Portland Street W1N

Greenford UB6

Purley CR8

Seven Sisters N4

Vauxhall SW8

## MOTORCYCLE City

### TRAINING VOUCHER

# 10%OFF

## All Motorcycle City Training Courses –

### save up to

# £50

Motorcycle City Training offer a wide range of courses from Compulsory Basic Training (CBT) through Direct Access and Standard Full Licence courses to Advanced Training.

Use this voucher to save 10% of the cost of training (excluding bike-hire charges).

### Conditions
- The voucher must be used at the time of booking. Please advise the booking office that a voucher is to be used when you confirm your course.
- The voucher entitles the holder to a 10% reduction in the price of any motorcycle training course.
- It cannot be used against bike hire not included within a course, or against the cost of a motorcycle test.